UP AND DOWN
UNDER

By the same author

Dougal Haston: The Philosophy of Risk

UP AND DOWN
UNDER

THE INSIDE STORY OF THE
2001 BRITISH LIONS TOUR
OF AUSTRALIA

JEFF CONNOR

CANONGATE

First published in Great Britain in 2001 by
Canongate Books Ltd, 14 High Street,
Edinburgh EH1 1TE

10 9 8 7 6 5 4 3 2 1

British Library Cataloguing-in-Publication Data
A catalogue record for this book is available on
request from the British Library

ISBN 1 84195 211 7

Typeset by Palimpsest Book Production Limited,
Polmont, Stirlingshire

Printed and bound by
Creative Print and Design, Ebbw Vale, Wales

www.canongate.net

CONTENTS

FOREWORD

By Finlay Calder OBE

Captain of the successful 1989 British Lions in Australia

The 2001 British and Irish Lions set off for Australia in a mood of great optimism. Many said this could be the greatest Lions squad ever to leave these shores and there was talk of an overwhelming series win. We forgot two things: the Lions were playing the undisputed world champions in their own backyard and that there is much more to a successful tour than assembling outstanding playing talent.

As the tour unfolded, it became clear that something, somewhere, was going horribly wrong. Apart from a devastating catalogue of injuries to key players there were rumours of behind-the-scenes bickering and player discontent and, of course, history ultimately will tell us that the Lions failed.

For me, the defining moment came at the end of the Third Test in Sydney's wonderful Stadium Australia when the Lions captain Martin Johnson, a massive figure on and off the field, signed off by thanking his players and the team's amazing travelling support. As we have come to expect from Martin, he did not seek scapegoats or excuses, but he did confirm that lovely old expression: 'If you can't say anything good about someone, say nothing.' He said nothing about the 2001 Lions management.

It seemed from the outset that the personal ambitions of some of the management team far outweighed their ambition for the success of the players. The players were simply vehicles for their own agendas and this proved a gross error of misjudgment. A good employer always puts his staff first.

I have immense sympathy for the players of today, however

well paid they may be. Too much is being asked of them and it became clear in Australia that at least half of the squad were worn out, mentally and physically. The fierce training regime there merely exacerbated that condition. It's easy to discipline players who spoke out against this, but the management should have remembered: You may not like the message, but don't shoot the messenger.

In time, the four Home Unions will sit down and discuss what went wrong and attempt to get things right for New Zealand 2005. Perhaps, for starters, they should consider some bedtime reading and buy Jeff Connor's latest book covering the occasional ups and lots of the downs in Australia. Jeff has a perceptive mind, and has always demonstrated to me that he is unwilling to take things at face value. His funny, and yet occasionally very sad, story of the 2001 Lions tour hopefully will open a few eyes about modern professional rugby.

FINLAY CALDER
Lauder
July 2001

ACKNOWLEDGMENTS

Sincere thanks go to Dave Gibson of Fotosport for his superb pictures of the 2001 British and Irish Lions tour and his moral support and friendship in Australia. This book would certainly have not been possible without the backing of my employers at Scotland on Sunday and my gratitude goes to them, in particular Paul Greaves. Duggie Middleton, once again, was an astute editor and the enthusiasm, patience and faith of Jamie Byng, David Graham and particularly Mark Stanton at Canongate have never failed to be anything but inspiring.

Finally, Australia was made far brighter by the presence of Finlay Calder, and I am also indebted to him for his foreword and for reading the final manuscript.

INTRODUCTION

This book is a purely personal view of what went on during the 2001 British and Irish Lions tour of Australia. There are others far better qualified to say where it all went wrong on the field and why the Lions failed to upset the Wallabies in their own lair and I have not attempted to do that.

Like many of the players this was my first tour – and probably after this book my last – and I approached it with what I now recognise as laughable naivety. The overwhelming excitement and disbelief when it was decided that I would be travelling ten thousand miles on one of the greatest sporting assignments possible has not quite evaporated even now, but it is probably true to say that I am slightly more cynical about the ideals behind a Lions tour, and the absurb concept of a hundred or so professional journalists pursuing fifty professional rugby players and their staff around a vast continent to report their deeds. Particularly when many of those players, and almost all of their management, plainly wished those journalists were elsewhere.

Before setting out and after reading so much about the Lions in the past I had foolishly imagined some wholesome conglomerate of press and players and management sailing serenely around Australia like a particularly jolly cruise ship. I sincerely hoped that I would return home on first-name terms with some of the squad and on head coach Graham Henry's Christmas card list. In reality the 2001 British and Irish Lions tour was conducted under a metaphorical banner which read 'Winning Is Everything', a dogma that put relations with the press, British and Australian, at the bottom of a long list of priorities. Nor were there many attempts to win over the local populace;

the notion that a Lions tour was a benign mission to spread the gospel of rugby had been discarded somewhere between Heathrow Airport and Perth, Western Australia. No one blames the Lions management for this; they had a forbidding workload and a difficult job to do in too short a time, and the press can be a nuisance at times. But any justifications vanished with defeat in Stadium Australia and perhaps it would have been better to have had a happy losing tour than a miserable losing tour. There also appeared to be a lot of people with their own agendas, most of which involved some measure of commercialism. Priorities were lost and if the Lions tour committee are seeking answers to what went wrong they could do worse than examine the varying motives of a few of the Lions party – and those of all the Wallabies.

Some very funny moments were enjoyed on tour and some extremely rewarding ones. The efforts and ultimate failure of Martin Johnson and his men in the defeat in the final Test in Sydney was moving and arousing in equal measure. And anyone who doesn't consider a free seat to watch a three-match Test series between the world champions and the British and Irish Lions a major highlight in a career doesn't deserve to be there in the first place. But it was a very odd trip.

JEFF CONNOR
Edinburgh
August 2001

ONLY A GAME

As the late Clem Thomas pointed out in his definitive history of the British Lions, the first tour, to Australia and New Zealand in 1888, was organised and operated not by the four Home Unions but by private promoters, two impresarios who not only saw the opportunity of spreading the gospel of rugby to the colonies, but the chance to make a few bob – or at least to break even. In the 113 years since, there have been tours of varying length, fluctuating results and differing opposition. Those trailblazers played fifty-three matches in all with only twenty-two players and were away for eight months. The tour began with the disqualification of one of the party for professionalism and another was drowned in the Hunter River. The comparisons with their 2001 antecedents are obvious and possibly simplistic, but one statistic about the 1888 tour did find a modern counterpart: the 2001 version was also indisputably a major commercial operation, run by entrepreneurs for whom the sport of rugby was simply a means to an end. The famous jersey with that heart-shaped badge made up of the logos of the four Home Unions, the wearing of which players since 1888 had come to regard as the ultimate reward in rugby union, had become a marketable commodity.

The Lions tour committee, through their chairman, the former British Lions player and coach Dr Syd Millar MBE, are extremely protective of the marketing potential of the Lions badge as those who have sought to use it for personal gain, or even in the cause of charity, have found to their cost. The shield's copyright had been registered in 1997, at a cost of twenty thousand pounds, for future commercial use, in the main the royalties from sales of replica jerseys and other souvenirs. The new fiscal policies of the Lions tour committee do not sit easily with players and administrators

1

of an earlier vintage, but none would ever kid themselves that the four Home Unions and the Lions committee would have the capability, or desire, to put up the estimated three million pounds needed to send the 2001 tourists to Australia and maintain them there for seven weeks. Players and coaches have to be paid, fed and watered and with a party some fifty-strong that does not come cheaply. The players' wage bill alone – the thirty-seven selected could earn a maximum of twenty-eight thousand pounds each – came to one million pounds.

The previous Lions tour to South Africa in 1997, the first of the professional era, lost around four hundred thousand pounds and the cost had been met by the Home Unions. They quite rightly wanted to avoid a repeat. England, the most commercially astute, or maybe greedy, of the Home Unions also hinted that they may, if not on this trip at least in the future, demand a bigger say in where tour-generated revenue went. Australia, while footing the bill for most of the Lions travel and hotel costs, retained all the TV rights, which at some four hundred million viewers worldwide for each of the Tests, were of considerable importance. England, however, provided eighteen of the 2001 Lions squad and, as had happened over Six Nations TV rights, the English Rugby Football Union were not slow to discover an injustice in this and began flexing their muscles.

Chief executive Francis Baron said: 'Lions matches are controlled by the host unions and that is a bone of contention for us. We believe that the Lions is such a strong brand that it should control its own rights. We should at least divide the money between the host and participating unions. At the moment we get no share of the TV money, no share of the gates or sponsorship. It is not a sensible way forward. TV rights are worth a lot to Australia and the four Home Unions need a cut. In future, the Lions needs a change in thinking so we all get that.'

As the RFU also plaintively pointed out they had also lost to the Lions the services of their kicking coach Dave Aldred, forwards coach Andy Robinson and defensive expert Phil Larder. With a tour of Canada coinciding with the Lions in Australia these three key figures in the English hierarchy had to be replaced – at a cost. All this may make commercial sense in sport's new golden days, but there were times in the early summer of 2001 when one wondered if the forthcoming tour was about playing rugby or simply making money and brown-nosing sponsors. Even Millar, one of the great Lions, sounded baffled at times by the demands of the professional era and when asked at a press conference how the Lions intended to raise the three million pounds required for the 2001 tour, he admitted: 'With great difficulty!'

Apart from the business of making a profit or breaking even and perhaps in between winning the series against Australia, undeniably something else was at stake; the very existence of the Lions. With the popularity of the World Cup and the increasing demands put on players there had been doubts expressed about this even before the South African tour of 1997. Some club owners, the men who paid the wages, saw touring as an unnecessary intrusion into a player's season that was growing ever longer. More sponsors and more competitions had appeared culminating in the Zurich Premiership play-offs a fortnight before the Lions flew out to Perth. Austin Healey, to quote one example, had played over fifty games by the time the tour came round and was being asked to fly ten thousand miles to face men who had played less than thirty and were only halfway through their season.

The 1997 tour, as it turned out, had been a watershed; victory over the Springboks and the large number of travelling fans had won the Lions a reprieve from the pragmatists. A losing series four years later and the calls for the Lions to be disbanded and packed off into the history books would almost certainly resurface.

During the weeks preceding departure for Australia on Friday June 1, a bewildering variety of messages via

3

traditional press handout or via e-mail began to land on the desks or surface in the computers of journalists who would be travelling Down Under with the British and Irish Lions. These included reminders that Caffreys was the official beer of the 2001 tour, Land Rover would provide the transport and that adidas were the main outfitters. There were welcome invitations from Zurich Financial Services to booze-ups in Melbourne and golfing days on the Gold Coast and from adidas to a barbie and beach rugby on Fairweather Beach, close to Manly. Confirmations arrived from the Australian Rugby Union about accreditation, visas and advice on the Lions' pre-tour activities from their media liaison manager Alex Broun. We received a media stats pack, a survival guide from our selected tour companies and, eventually, the cherished travel pack containing tickets for two external and eight internal flights, hotel vouchers . . . and dire warnings about the effects of in-flight DVT. Most of the mail, however, came on high-quality, double-strength notepaper bearing the Lions shield alongside a larger logo that read NTL.

The TV, telephone and broadband Internet company, whose sponsorship portfolio included Newcastle, Aston Villa, Celtic and Rangers football clubs, had paid one million pounds for the use of the Lions badge and the chance to employ it to advertise their various communications services. Their aim was to get 'up close and personal with the Lions' and their involvement included access for fans to tour statistics and news on the Internet, a link-up with Sky Sports and digital TV coverage and video diaries by individual players. As Donal Lenihan, the tour manager, put it: 'This really will become known as the Tour of Technology'.

For their million pounds NTL also earned the right to have a foot-high logo on the Lions jerseys, leisure wear and training tops. With the adidas symbol on the other side and the traditional Lions badge fighting for space in between, the cherished Lions red jersey was beginning to look as overcrowded as the front of Michael Schumacher's racing overalls. As most of the twenty thousand Lions fans in Australia insisted on showing their loyalties by purchasing replica jerseys at fifty pounds a throw the NTL investment was soon beginning to look the biggest bargain since the Dutch paid the Mohawks sixty guilders for Manhattan Island.

NTL reportedly were some eleven billion pounds in debt at the time of the 2001 Lions tour and had just made five thousand staff in the UK redundant as part of a cost-cutting exercise and they understandably set about getting some return for their investment through their nominated marketing agents, Octagon.

The resultant sponsorship knock-ons sold by Octagon appeared as tangled and incestuous as the Borgia family tree. Aspect TV, an independent company in Wales earned the contract to make a fly-on-the-wall documentary on the Lions tour although the rights and presumably most of the profits remained with NTL and the video publishers, Lace International. In South Africa four years previously a similar documentary was filmed and broadcast on ITV and Sky and later released on two videos, *Living with the Lions* 1 and *Living with the Lions* 2. The first of these and the only justification for the second – proved to be one of the biggest-selling sports videos of all time with buyers attracted to what was basically a soap opera. There was raw, earthy language from the players, rantings of coaches, the previously unseen view of what went on in dressing rooms and some very moving moments, particularly when injured players were told their tour was over. There was high drama when medics fought to bring round the concussed centre Will Greenwood and the sales were also helped indisputably by the fact that the 1997 Lions managed a rare series victory over the then world champions.

The Aspect film crew four years later hoped to emulate all this and made some optimistic noises about their involvement. They would fly to Australia with the players, stay at the same hotel and 'spend every waking hour with them'.

5

The producer promised: 'Graham Henry said they will be up at 5.30 a.m. every day to work out in the gym and said I should go along, too.'

In 1997, the coaching duo of Jim Telfer and Ian McGeechan, and a large number of the players, had been far from happy about this sort of intrusion. Previously a Lions dressing room had been inviolate both before and after a match and in 1993 a request by London Weekend to make a fly-on-the-wall documentary of the tour of New Zealand had been rejected as being too invasive. Four years later the sport had staggered into the professional era and anything was for sale. Suddenly, the players' every deed – embarrassing male-bonding, throwing up, bashing heads on dressing room walls and all the F-words – were in the public eye and ear. Much as they may have blanched at it, Telfer and McGeechan had to put up with all this for a simple reason; a film company had bought the rights and the Lions committee had signed the contract.

In 2001 there was scarcely a murmur from the head coach Graham Henry, but then here is a man who certainly recognises commercial reality. He and his wife Raewyn, until sponsorship fell through, had their own website which contained chatty news updates about their lives – and special offers for his autobiography. On the Australian tour he was being paid for a newspaper column and had also negotiated a deal through his ghost writer Nick Bishop to tell his story of the 2001 tour in a book, Bishop keeping the advance and Henry pocketing any subsequent royalties. Although in his mid-fifties there was little doubt that the Lions coach was a child of the professional era.

Aspect undoubtedly arrived with Henry's recommendation. They had trailed him when he returned to New Zealand and the subsequent documentary *Away at Home*, was screened in the run-up to the 1999 World Cup. Aspect also produced *Graham Henry's Six Nations*, which was broadcast by BBC Wales. The film company and the Welsh coach were old pals.

Apart from the hand-held Aspect cameras there were also plans for webcams in the dressing room and on the team bus, while daily video diaries by the players would feature on the NTL website. Ieuan Evans, former Wales captain and 1989 was, in the words of an NTL hand-out, to 'seek out more fly-on-the-wall material while in Australia'. *Big Brother* was never like this and NTL's advertising jingle 'What goes on tour now goes on TV' was spot on.

Not all the Octagon deals went as smoothly. It had been agreed that the national photographic agency, Allsport, would be the 'official' photographers through their man-on-the-spot, Dave Rogers. Rogers would be allowed full access to every training session while the rest of the snappers were shooed away after twenty minutes or so. As can be imagined, this caused some degree of ill-feeling and when Rogers had all his equipment nicked from Manly beach there wasn't exactly a lot of sympathy wafted in his direction. His photographic colleagues may not have raised three cheers, but much behind-the-hand sniggering was detected.

There were other money squabbles, notably between rival sports websites keen to cash in on the appeal of the Lions. The new media rights – NTL were concentrating on their broadband activities – had been offered to Scrum.com, a subsidiary of Sportal and were to host the 'official' site, lionstour.com. This did not go down too well with Rugbee.com, who held the new media rights to a number of the squad members, including Jonny Wilkinson and Matt Dawson. Director Andy Clarke, who with his brother Phil, the former Great Britain rugby league international, ran Rugbee.com, said that he was 'concerned' about what would happen with the players during the tour, and insisted that his company should be able to 'protect our assets'. The old concept of players going on tour to take part in rugby matches again seemed to have fallen by the wayside as Clarke added: 'We're not sure what will happen. We have these exclusive rights and obviously we want to exercise them. We don't want to cause problems but it'll be interesting to see what happens.'

Where there is money and sponsorship in sport there are also free-loaders – journalists, please note, do some occasional work – and NTL were also footing the bill for a gang of rugby-loving MPs to fly out on their own tour of Australia. The twenty-five politicians naturally claimed they were on a 'fact-finding' visit – to places like Sydney Opera House and the Great Barrier Reef – and the fifteen-thousand-pounds-a-head trip incurred the wrath of, among others, the Tory MP John Redwood who said: 'This tour means the MPs are missing practically all of what is a very short summer sitting. It is over the top.'

The Honourable Members played against Australian teams in between taking in most of the Lions games and their spokesman, the Leicester Labour MP Andy Reed, reported gamely: 'We are all working extremely hard out here. I'm probably doing longer hours than I usually do.' So politics and sport do mix.

And then there were the boys and girls from Octagon, the NTL agents. The sports marketing specialist have offices in thirty-six cities worldwide, including London and Sydney, and fingers in a lot of sporting pies. They handle the affairs of tennis players Martina Hingis and Elena Dokic and also ran Club Octagon, 'the most exciting internet club of its kind in the world of motorsport'. The company also held exclusive rights to capitalise on the commercial potential of chess worldwide; in rugby, they were heavily involved in the Heineken Cup and the Six Nations. On the tour of Australia they were represented by a bewildering and ever-changing number of employees, whose functions remained extremely vague. One had the daily, admittedly extremely boring, job of assembling and dissembling the portable backdrop covered in sponsors' logos at the daily press conference, but many of the others – particularly the younger males – simply wandered around in British Lions leisure gear trying to look like British Lions.

Some of Octagon's view of their own worth can be gathered from one of their travelling employees, who when asked to describe her working day, said: 'My main role is liaison with sponsors, which is vital to the success of any Lions tour.' In other words, keeping NTL, Caffreys, adidas, Zurich and Land Rover happy was as necessary to the 2001 series as Brian O'Driscoll's sidestep, Richard Hill's tackling and Jonny Wilkinson's left boot.

In terms of bending the knee to sponsors, the Lions of 2001 were not unique. The Wallabies had negotiated multi-million-dollar five-year deals with Vodafone and Bundaberg Rum and anyone attending a sporting event there could not fail to notice that in terms of hammering the consumer over the head with non-stop advertising Australia leaves even the United States far behind. If not, the words of none other than John O'Neill, chief executive of the Australian Rugby Union, writing in the 2001 Wallabies handbook will do: 'The Bundaberg Rum Rugby Test Series incorporates the three Lions Tests and the Tri-Nations series. Please get familiar with those titles and feel free to get familiar with Bundaberg Rum; that way we will all get a warm inner glow.'

After all the financial manoeuvrings, nothing else much had changed about the protocol of a Lions tour and the two years before departure it followed the time-honoured guide-lines. Official acceptance of the invitation from Australia had been made and another invitation from the Lions Committee had gone out to all four Home Unions asking them to nominate a manager, coach and assistant coach. When these were selected there followed a few months of wrangling over the itinerary – always a great point of debate – before the final dates and venues were confirmed. Finally, all that was left was to find a squad of players capable of beating the best rugby union side in the world on their own turf.

JOHNNO AND CO

The manager and captain of the 2001 Lions virtually picked themselves. The choice of the head coach turned out to be somewhat more contentious.

The former Ireland captain and Lion Donal Lenihan, a tourist in 1983, 1986 and 1989 and at the time of his appointment, in charge of the Ireland national side, was an almost unanimous choice as manager by Millar and the Lions committee – despite Millar's insistence that 'there were a number of outstanding candidates'. The appointment was announced in early February, 2000 and the recruitment of the big, handsome and urbane Munsterman seemed a wise move. His daytime job as an administrator with Irish Permanent Building Society and undoubted commercial skills would help. Lenihan knew how, and when, to say yes and no.

He had a hard act to follow after the success of Fran Cotton in South Africa four years earlier when the former England prop had not only guided the Lions to a series victory but also wiped the floor with the South African and British media and Springbok administrators. The contrast in styles would certainly be illuminating. Cotton could be confrontational and abrasive; Lenihan, with his armoury of witty one-liners, preferred killing with charm although he did have a similar imposing physical presence to his predecessor.

Lenihan was born in Cork in 1959. His father, Ger, was a noted Gaelic footballer and All-Ireland Irish heavyweight boxing champion – 'I always tell people that in case someone fancies a go some night' – but the young Lenihan preferred rugby. He spent all of his playing career with Cork Constitution, the appositely named club based at Temple Hill, where the disposition of an ox was often needed to survive the shenanigans on, and off, the field. His Test debut

10

in the Irish second row came in 1981 – against Australia and he went on to gain fifty-two caps, winning a Triple Crown in 1982 and 1985 and captaining his country seventeen times. But it was his role as captain of the midweek Lions side on the tour of 1989 which was the most relevant item on his CV to Millar and his selection panel. Although he was only captain on three occasions Lenihan's role as the cheery leader of 'Donal's Donuts' has gone down into Lions folklore as an example of how a happy, successful midweek side – the dirt trackers – can influence a whole tour in a positive fashion. Oddly, this lesson was not carried over into the tour of 2001. Or if it was, it was quickly discarded.

Although a man of great magnetism and wit, Lenihan was not universally popular with some sections of the Irish press. Some saw him as ambitious – 'Donal considers the political expediency of which side of the bed he gets out of bed every morning' as one put it – and surmised that a Lions victory in Australia would smooth his passage to a post on the International Rugby Board, based in Dublin. But this was hardly considered a disqualifying factor for an administrator in the professional era. Everyone had their own agendas and even his most cynical critics could hardly argue with Lenihan's qualifications to manage. There were, however, question marks over his ability as a media performer and his ability to stand up to the strident Aussieisms he would face on a daily basis Down Under. Some saw the soft-spoken manner and the *'tises* and *'twases* as West Cork whimsy and that the Aussies would make mincemeat of him. In the event, they were his biggest weapons.

After his appointment Lenihan had only eighteen months before the Lions set out and an awful lot on his plate. It was an awesome responsibility and a forbidding workload. His first job was to get the management team and coaching staff on board, along with the medical and back-up people. Then there was the selection process and the contractual negotiations with the players. The itinerary had to be debated and agreed with the Australian Rugby Union and accommodation and training facilities inspected and approved. Host Unions traditionally like to soften up a touring team early on with two or three confrontational provincial matches and engender some additional strain with fixtures spread, geographically, as wide as possible. Tour managements are as equally determined to work out a careful schedule of escalating difficulty with a modicum of packing and unpacking in between.

There was also a potential problem with referees; all the officials nominated for the Test series were drawn from the southern hemisphere – two South Africans and a New Zealander – and the problem for the Lions was that they were used to refereeing week in, week out, at Super 12 level. When Lenihan said that 'therefore they probably have a better working relationship with the southern hemisphere players' the implication was obvious. He would also have to establish some sort of dialogue with them.

Lenihan's toughest tasks, however, he admitted before departure, would be the day-to-day man-management of the players, the breaking of news to the injured that their tour was over and the necessity of attempting to keep the malcontents left out of the Test side reasonably happy. There were also the daily demands of an unprecedented army of media, all with their individual needs and deadlines. None of these aspects of the job filled Lenihan with anything approaching joyful expectation.

Lenihan's first choice as head coach had been Ian McGeechan of Scotland who already boasted series wins in Australia in 1989 and in South Africa in 1997 and a near miss in New Zealand in 1993. Widely regarded as one of the most astute operators in the business and universally popular with players and press, McGeechan had also experienced two tours as a player and his qualifications were unquestionable. He had, however, just begun a long-term contract with the Scottish national team, a formidable assignment, as players and administrators north of the border had hardly slipped smoothly into the professional era. Despite Lenihan's extended pleadings McGeechan turned the opportunity down, stayed in Scotland and the 2001 Lions manager had to look elsewhere.

There was only one other viable British candidate – the England coach Clive Woodward, who had taken over after Jack Rowell's resignation in the autumn of 1997 and in the four years since could boast victories against South Africa (twice), Argentina and Australia. The former international centre had also succeeded in transforming England's traditional forward-dominated playing style into something more expansive and in the Six Nations campaign of 2001 they had played a brand of rugby seldom seen in that competition with crushing victories over Wales and Scotland. But there had also been a few hiccups. The quarter-final defeat by South Africa during the 1999 World Cup, when he had left out the English golden boy Jonny Wilkinson and paid the penalty, had led to fierce criticism and there had been some spectacular last-gasp slip-ups to Wales (coached by Graham Henry) and Scotland (coached by McGeechan) in 1999 and 2000. The defeat at Wembley by an inspired Welsh side and the spectacular mugging at Murrayfield a year later had cost England two Grand Slams.

Nor was Woodward, with his revolutionary methods, outspoken attitude and insistence on becoming involved in virtually every rugby debate going, everyone's cup of tea. Some thought him too far too cocky for his own good. In the end he was not even approached for the Lions job. Among the coaches of the four Home Unions that left only the itinerant New Zealanders – Warren Gatland of Ireland and Henry of Wales. Gatland was considered far too inexperienced at international level, and although his Irish side had given every indication that they could give England a good run for their money in the 2001 Six Nations, he had a couple of sticky seasons before that. At one point he had been on the verge of being sacked, presumably by Lenihan.

13

And then there was one . . .

No one could argue with Henry's credentials. The former headmaster of Kelston Boy's High School in Auckland had coached Auckland Blues to two Super 12 titles and won eighty out of one hundred and two matches in New Zealand's National Provincial Championship. When he took over as Welsh coach in 1998 he put together ten consecutive victories and achieved a first-ever victory over South Africa, in 1999. He was regarded as both meticulous and innovative and was popular with his Welsh players and the press. In 1999, when he made his first trip to Murrayfield he captivated most observers with his candour, graciousness and intelligent summing-up of Wales's 33–20 defeat. 'Crikey, we were bloody lucky to come second,' he said at the time. At his interview by the Welsh Rugby Union in Cardiff in July 1998, he had been perceived as a breath of fresh air with his mixture of charm, pragmatism and persuasiveness, only his salary demands causing the panel to choke on their digestive biscuits. He had been welcomed as the Great Redeemer by a success-starved Welsh rugby public.

There were quite a few buts, however. His estimated two hundred and fifty thousand pounds annual wage package had taken some at the WRU, and the Welsh public, aback and by 2001 the initial surge of success had run out of steam. There had been crushing reverses against England and France and physically it appeared that he was beginning to feel the pressure. It had been remarked that he had visibly aged in the three years since his appointment; the brow was more furrowed, the complexion more florid, the speech less lucid and the demeanor more defensive.

In the press conference following the monumentally one-sided 15–44 defeat by England at the Millennium Stadium early in 2001 Henry looked like a rabbit caught in car headlights unable, or unwilling, to grasp the nature of the butchery out on the field. In the background, the knives were being sharpened. Former Wales internationals

Jonathan Davies and Gerald Davies were among those who questioned Henry's record and his selection policy – like many New Zealand coaches he preferred bulk to outright pace in the backs, a strategy badly exposed by England and, Davies went so far as to say that Henry's record compared unfavourably with the discarded former national coaches, Kevin Bowring and Alan Davies. Others pointed out that his successes with Auckland had been achieved with some of the greatest of contemporary All Black players, including Grant Fox, Sean Fitzpatrick, Jonah Lomu and Zinzan and Robin Brooke.

His autocratic coaching methods – while Henry plugged away virtually alone other countries had a small army of defensive coaches, forward coaches and kicking coaches – were suddenly seen as old-fashioned. When Henry said the whole coaching infrastructure in Wales needed overhauling many wondered what he had been doing for the last three years.

There were also mutterings about Grannygate, critics insisting that he encouraged the New Zealand flanker Brett Sinkinson and Henry's former Auckland full-back Shane Howarth to invent their Welsh ancestries, and his habit of last-minute substitutions – players could claim appearance money and a cap – was attributed to a mercenary mindset. He had never taken up the offer of a contract with the New Zealand Rugby Union because he was miffed that players were paid more than coaches. Many in Wales felt that on his salary and the faith the WRU had shown in him, Henry like McGeechan, should have been concentrating on the long-term future of the country he coached, rather than the Lions.

McGeechan's rationale for refusing another tour as coach read almost like a condemnation of Henry's appointment, the Scotland coach saying: 'The Lions will always be important to me and that's why I considered the offer of coaching them next year in Australia very seriously. But with the autumn Tests and 2001 Six Nations ahead I felt coaching

15

the Lions could lead to me doing neither that job nor my Scotland one justice. I looked hard to see if I could balance the two roles, but I wasn't convinced I could be in control of both jobs at the same time. Lions tours are unique and special occasions, and it's a tremendous privilege to have coached them three times. The temptation to make it four was increased by the presence of Donal Lenihan as manager, because he's a super person. But in the end I felt I couldn't give the Lions the time and preparation they'd need without compromising my job with Scotland. As a coach you still need to know all about the planning, and from that develop a criterion for the type of player needed. Whoever does coach the Lions must have the respect of the players. The rugby strengths of each country in Britain and Ireland are different and the Lions coach has to have an appreciation of what each country can bring to the table.'

The most oft-repeated criticism of Henry's appointment, however, centred on the fact that for the first time in Lions history the tour would be dependent on the coaching ability of an outsider. Most of the criticism came from former Lions players and coaches who believed that a New Zealander would have no concept of the tradition and history of the team and that it was setting a very dangerous precedent. This, even though there was at the time a Swedish football manager in charge of England, an Australian in charge of the Great Britain rugby league side and a Zimbabwean running the English cricket team. Even Mrs Henry was running the Cardiff netball team. If Henry failed to win the series in Australia, however, the chorus of 'Told you so's' would be deafening.

Henry had to break another habit of a lifetime when his selection was announced. It was obvious that this was certainly one job he could not handle on his own – in Wales he had only one assistant coach and he would have to learn how to employ and work with the bewildering army of backroom staff considered necessary for any modern, professional, international touring team. Based on the qualifications of men working for the various home nations the choice was not too difficult and just before Christmas 2000 Henry named his back-up. The assistant coaches in Australia were to be Andy Robinson, who would have charge of the Lions forwards and Phil Larder, who took responsibility for the defence. The kicking coaching would be in the hands, or feet, of Dave Alred who, like Robinson and Larder was a part of Woodward's successful England set-up.

Robinson, 37, had the advantage of having toured Australia with Lenihan in 1989 and as well as appearing for Bath in seven Twickenham cup winning teams from 1987 to 1996 represented England in eight Tests from 1988 to 1995. After retirement he turned to coaching and took over at Bath before his move into the England fold, first as assistant to Woodward and then as head coach when Woodward was moved to the post of manager. He had won a deserved reputation as an intelligent operator with a big work ethic which probably dated from his playing days. Like Neil Back, it was felt that his size – around 5ft 10in – had always been against him and he had to make up for this with a ferocious work rate. In one Twickenham programme the editor had said that 'Andy would be covering every piece of grass on the pitch' prompting the ultimate wind-up from the opposing Scotland back-row opponent who took great delight in pointing out to Robinson at every line-out: 'Look Andy there's a blade of grass you've missed.'

Robinson was also a dedicated early morning jogger – an almost infallible indication of a man who doesn't consider there are enough hours in a day.

Larder had played union for Broughton Park, Manchester and Sale before signing as a professional rugby league player with home-town Oldham in 1968. He moved on to Whitehaven in West Cumbria, a traditional graveyard for declining league players. Curiously, although his title with England and the Lions was defence coach his career in league had been notable for a lack of this ability. As

17

one former player rather uncharitably put it: 'You could go round Phil on the outside or sidestep him inside and if all else failed you'd just run straight over him.'

Larder had studied at Loughborough University and these unusual (for rugby league) cerebral qualities had given him a notable career as a coach, culminating with a spell as assistant to Great Britain coach Malcolm Reilly before taking charge of the British Lions league side that toured Papua New Guinea, Fiji and New Zealand in 1996. In the mid-1990s it had become almost de rigueur for national rugby union sides to plunder league for playing and coaching talent and in 1997 Larder became England's first adviser on defence, where his abilities made the team the meanest side in the northern hemisphere.

The official management team numbered thirteen, one more than Cotton and McGeechan had employed four years earlier and the 2001 backroom staff included some of the veterans of that tour including doctor James Robson, physio Mark Davies and masseur Andy Wegrzyk. Robson, a partner in a large medical practice in Dundee, is also a trained physiotherapist and was on his third tour, having first accompanied the Lions to New Zealand in 1993. He had been the undoubted star of the *Living with Lions* video in South Africa with his obvious caring involvement with the players. He had also been the centrepiece of some tearful footage when he had to tell players like Doddie Weir and Rob Howley that their tours were over. But his wife had also never let him forget his language, captured for posterity by the film's sound recordists.

Lenihan, like Cotton before him, has also recruited some familiar faces and Joan Moore, who worked as administrative secretary to the Irish national team, and baggage man Pat O'Keefe, a former Munster team official and fellow member of Cork Constitution, joined the 2001 tour.

Henry, too, had an input in the tried and trusted department. He brought in his former Welsh fitness adviser, an extraordinary character called Steve Black and Alun Carter, the former Pontypool and Newport flanker who ran his own business as a video analyst. Carter's role on tour entailed hour upon hour of winding and rewinding tapes of matches for the coaches and players to analyse later. Lenihan was to christen him Terry Waite 'because he never comes out of his room'.

Black had come to prominence with the rise of Newcastle Falcons to a Premiership title win in 1998 and he had been one of Henry's early recruits for his new Welsh set-up. The partnership lasted no more than eighteen months before Black resigned, claiming he had been made a scapegoat for poor results, the less-than-perfect physical state of the Quinnell brothers Craig and Scott, and the controversy surrounding Henry over the Grannygate affair. Black was big on principles; he had also quit Fulham when his good friend Paul Bracewell, the manager, was fired.

His actual role on tour was hard to define, although there was no doubting his value for many of the squad. Even he struggled to describe his *modus operandi* and perhaps the best job description is that of the tour's Feelgood Coordinator. In other words, when players felt down they went to see 'Blackie', who with his permanent, grin – like a synchronised swimmer – would do his best to cheer them up.

An open-faced, friendly 45-year-old Geordie with the solidity of the heavyweight boxer and weightlifter that he was he had attended the same Newcastle school as Sting and Neil Tennant of Pet Shop Boys and, after a spell at Newcastle United as a professional footballer, he followed his father and uncle into the pro fighting ranks before finding his metier as a coach. In Australia he organised much of the training and had the responsibility for players' weight-training. He was quite disparaging about their abilities in this direction: 'My two sons only weigh about thirteen stones and they are far better pound for pound'.

Black's extraordinary working day would start at around 6.30a.m. with tea in Henry's room before he delivered a handwritten note to every single player, telling them what was expected of them that day and how to reach their individual goals. He left nothing to chance: 'I find out as much as I can about the players beforehand, and try to get to know them and as much about the environment I am working in as I can. I then gel the unique characteristics and abilities within the group – whether coaches, administrators or the players – so they all feel they are playing their part, and then we press forward together with a shared goal.' Black, like Lenihan and Henry and all the players, had his own ambitions and goals, admitting: 'The best players in the world are here, and when you think about it, there is no equivalent in football, is there? There are fantastic opportunities here, and it is something I want to take advantage of. I need to know I have had an influence on the tour, and there is no way I can allow myself not to have had an influence, and I must keep hammering away. Everything's all about winning in the end.'

The final member of this odd, cosmopolitan mix of people dedicated to knocking over the Wallabies was an Australian, the media relations manager Alex Broun and of all the extremely industrious and dedicated backroom staff there is little doubt that he had the most thankless job of all.

Broun, like Black, had enjoyed a career of startling diversity. He had written plays and appeared as an actor in a number of Australian television shows, most notably *Neighbours*, where he played Brad the Butcher and had allegedly snogged Kylie Minogue, a story that raised his street cred among some journalists and cynical disbelief among the more jealous of us. Broun had also been a question in the Australian version of *Trivial Pursuit*: 'Who was Charlene's [Kylie Minogue's] first boyfriend?' The answer was not Jason Donovan but Brad the Butcher. Not surprisingly, the Broun and Brad story became favourite diary fodder for desperate rugby hacks.

After *Neighbours*, Broun covered the 1995 World Cup for various news agencies before taking the post of media officer for the South African Rugby Football Union, which is where he first came across Lenihan. Ireland had toured there in 1997 and although they lost the rugby they won the punch-ups in a tempestuous tour, prompting some condemnatory noises from Broun about the Fighting Irish. This did not go down too well with the Ireland manager.

Broun's job with SARFU story ended in bizarre fashion when the then Springbok coach Nick Mallett was comprehensively stitched up by a young female reporter masquerading as a supporter. She had appeared at a Springboks training session carrying a couple of balls to be autographed and without a notebook or visible tape recorder. In an offguard moment Mallett let rip at the SARFU pricing system calling it 'absolutely ridiculous'. The story immediately made headlines all over South Africa, Mallett came close to being sacked and when SARFU hauled Broun over the coals he resigned. In view of this, and events on the Irish tour in 1997 no one was more surprised than Broun when, after contacting the Lions manager for a job on the tour of Australia, Lenihan said yes.

In February 2001, after three days in West Cork with Henry and Robinson, Lenihan named sixty-seven British and Irish players who signed an initial agreement that made them available to the 2001 tour squad. These were considered the best around at the time, but ultimate selection for the elite final thirty-seven would be influenced by form in the Six Nations. Much also would depend on how many players steered clear of injury in the end-of-season cup and play-off competitions. As it was, Lawrence Dallaglio – definitely a key man for the Lions – damaged a knee in the Zurich Premiership play-offs and other leading players, notably Jonny Wilkinson, Iain Balshaw and Mike Catt, were also carrying injuries when the final list was unveiled. Such was their importance to the Lions' plans that they were still named to travel in the hope that they would recover in time for the Wallaby Tests. Lenihan also had a stand-by list and with England and Wales on tour in North America and Japan respectively, it was thought that most of the cover for injured players would come from these two countries.

In the past Lions selections there is no doubt there had been an element of horse-trading with each Home Union keen to get their individual players on tour, but since the early 1990s and particularly since the game went professional in 1995 the desire to win a series overrode all nationalistic conceptions of how a touring party should be made up. As it was, the selection of eighteen Englishmen, almost half the party, surprised virtually no-one on the strength of their Six Nations dominance while foot-and-mouth disease impacted on the selection of Ireland players. All the other players from England, Scotland and Wales had managed to play four games in the Six Nations, whereas the Irish missed out on three internationals as well as their own domestic competition. The choice of ten Welsh players surprised many while Scotland's place in the order of things was summed up by their representation of three.

The players found out in reassuringly archaic ways. Scott Murray, the Scotland lock, was told by a Saracens team-mate and thought it was a wind-up. Rob Howley, with Sky cameras trained and waiting for his reaction, heard the news on television in his Cardiff home; Austin Healey had to rely on the thumbs-up from a Leicester journalist from the side of the training pitch. All said without exception that this was the pinnacle of their careers, the greatest honour in rugby and that they would give everything for the cause.

There were few surprises in selection or omission. Some were shoe-ins, like Howley, Richard Hill, Scott Quinnell and the young Irish centre Brian O'Driscoll, who two years previously had been taken to Australia as a 19-year-old by Lenihan and Ireland. The fledgling Scotland forward Simon Taylor made the party, a stroke of outrageous fortune in some eyes, but not to those of Lenihan who had seen him destroy Northampton in an European Cup tie for Edinburgh Reivers earlier in the season.

Scott Gibbs, the folk hero of 1997, had been discarded, but there was a place for the game's highest-profile recruit Jason Robinson, formerly of Wigan rugby league club, who hadn't even started a game for England, Woodward preferring the far less gifted Ben Cohen. Much of the media pre-tour interest centred on the small figure of Robinson, by some distance the most intriguing selection.

Observers of rugby league knew he had the twinkling feet of the lead man in *Riverdance* and an awesome power-to-weight ratio, which had served him in good stead in league where thirteen-stone wings have to take their turn at tackling sixteen-stone forwards. 'I don't think I've ever played against anyone smaller than me,' mused Robinson. The lad from Hunslet was also good tabloid material because of his previous incarnation as a rather unhappy drunk before meeting the former Wigan player Inga Tuigamala. and becoming a born-again Christian. 'I made the decision to change my life and I've never looked back,' said Robinson. 'I'm at peace with myself and happy with my faith. For one thing, I've not had a hangover for five and a half years. Before, there were many days, day after day after day, when I used to wake up wondering where I was.' Great player, but definitely a bit of an oddity in rugby union. At the other end of the scale the prop Dai Young, a veteran of the 1989 tour, was going back, older, much bigger and wiser. And he still liked a pint.

The main question for many observers south of the Border, east of the Wash and on the other side of the Irish Sea were how many non-Englishmen would get into the Test line-up, an error many had made in 1997 when some dark horses had come galloping up on the rails, notably the Scottish prop Tom Smith and the Ireland lock Jeremy Davidson – both selected again. Many thought that either Will Greenwood or Mike Catt would automatically partner O'Driscoll in the centre, ignoring the other claimants, notably Ireland's Rob Henderson who finished up starting all three Tests. Howley had had a marvellous season for Wales and his extra pace gave him the edge over Matt Dawson while at stand-off Jonny Wilkinson looked a certainty with Ronan O'Gara and Neil Jenkins resigned to back-up roles. The task of hooking and throwing in at the line-out were in the hands of another hero of 1997, Ireland's Keith Wood, with Phil Greening of England and Robin McBryde of Wales waiting in the wings. In the front row, Jason Leonard was on his third Lions tour and with Young added a touch of laddish sanity to the proceedings. There was an awful lot of competition for not many places.

One spot that was not open to other contenders, was on the left side of the second-row of the scrum. This belonged to the captain, Martin Johnson, unarguably the dominant figure on this tour and the last. There had been attempts to advance the claims of Wood to lead the Lions, but there was only really one candidate. Johnson had the experience of having done the job before in 1997 – and was undoubtedly the most fearsome man in British rugby. In South Africa, by all accounts, he had proved a superb leader without any measure of off-field warmth. Four years later, however, he was far more approachable. Almost friendly at times.

This mellowing, however, had not taken the ability of his frown to freeze at ten paces and interviewing Johnson would always occasion a certain amount of trepidation, even among the most hardened of hacks. Johnson was fresh, if that's the right word, from the longest season in rugby history and a third successive title win for his club Leicester, success in the Zurich Championship final and a final draining Heineken Cup victory against Stade Francais in Paris. He was, on past and current record and appearance and example the ultimate leader, the only question mark being over a disciplinary record that had seen him suspended for one Twickenham Test against South Africa in the autumn of 1997 after punching the All Black Justin Marshall in a previous match and a 35-day ban for kneeing the Saracens scrum-half Duncan McRae in the ribs early in 2001. The finest compliment anyone could pay Johnson was this: while lesser players consulted agents, discussed new contracts or wrote newspaper columns, Johnson was interested in only one thing – playing and winning, at rugby.

This, then, was the unlikely conglomerate of nationalities, values, beliefs and shapes and sizes charged with beating the world champions on their home patch. The task for Henry and his management was awesome: after a ten-thousand-mile journey to the other side of the world to a different climate, time zone and culture, there would be just six matches before the First Test in Brisbane. He would have to, in his own words, 'hit the ground running'. In terms of talent, he had arguably the strongest Lions squad ever assembled and the overwhelming feeling even before they set out was that the 2001 tourists could emulate those of 1989 and beat the Wallabies.

But Henry also had an awful lot of playing personnel for a ten-match, seven-week tour – the shortest ever. Basic mathematics would tell him that there would be some disappointments for a large number of players and as well as damage to egos there would be injuries and loss of form; the biggest problem for Henry, Lenihan, Black and the rest of the management team would be keeping everybody happy.

Then there were the Wallabies, or as they were known in their own land, 'the world champion Wallabies'. As the Lions and their management prepared for their initial coming-together Lenihan made no bones about the task of playing and defeating Australia – at anything: 'You almost have to be sitting down in the dressing room ten minutes after you've beaten them to be sure you actually have done it. They have that mental resolve that we are going to have to generate.'

And asked to define the quintessential Lions player the manager replied: 'Someone who, when he gets a kick in the bollocks, will stand up and come back.'

Unfortunately, the Lions did not hold the copyright on this trait of character and the Wallabies proved far more capable of taking a kick in the bollocks, standing up and coming back.

THE PLAYING FIELDS OF ALDERSHOT

Those who had read his first volume of autobiography (his second was timed to come out after the Lions won the series in Australia) were aware that the head coach was not the world's best at recalling dates or names. In *Graham Henry, the X-Factor*, he referred, among other gaffes, to the Scotland flanker Martin Leslie – a New Zealand countryman and from Auckland – as Martin Peters and called Martyn Williams, a man to whom he had awarded a first Welsh cap, Martin Williams. But nothing prepared the world for the galloping amnesia that characterised Henry's first major public appearance as Lions coach at Heathrow's Crowne Plaza at the end of May, 2001.

He couldn't put a name to the Ireland centre who was eventually to make three Test appearances (Rob Henderson), forgot the name of the referee in the Second Test (Jonathan Kaplan) and referred to the *Sunday Telegraph* writer Paul Ackford – a former British Lion himself and at 6ft 5in hardly unmistakable – as 'John'. He also admitted he 'hardly knew' his captain Martin Johnson and with the start of the tour a week away had only 'a couple of chats with him'. Henry was either the worst-prepared coach in Lions history or the biggest wind-up merchant of all time. Perhaps it had more to do with the traditional befuddlement of middle age – Henry would be fifty-five during the tour – and the feeling well known to many that while we can remember what happened thirty years ago we can't recall much of what occurred yesterday. Henry, at least, seemed to have bought into Lions history and could recall in glorious detail the 1959 tour of New Zealand and a party that included Gordon Wood, father of Keith.

'It was my first ever contact with the Lions,' said Henry. 'It was a marvellous attacking team hut never got its just desserts. and they were robbed of glory by the All Black full-back Don Clarke's boot. He kicked six penalty goals in the first Test to the Lions' four tries and the Lions went down 18–17. My father was embarrassed. It was the only time he ever admitted that the All Blacks didn't deserve to win.'

Henry could reel off all the names, too: Tony O'Reilly, Peter Jackson, Bev Risman, Roddie Evans and the man who had appointed Henry in the first place, Syd Millar chairman of the Lions committee. It was a fine performace and even those who had questioned the wisdom of appointing a foreigner to coach a British Isles team had been half-convinced. A week later, when the head coach got his players together for the first time, there was a sneaking feeling that the Lenihan and the Lions committee might just have chosen the right man after all.

The 2001 tour for the players was to begin officially with six days and nights at Tylney Hall, a gothic country pile close to Hook, in Hampshire. The vast touring entourage of players, management, coaches, baggage handlers, doctor and physios and various honorary hangers-on gathered there for the first time on Saturday May 26, for what turned out to be a heavily compressed week. The schedule included not only the initial twice-daily training sessions at nearby Aldershot, but a compulsory and sullenly anticipated media day in the hotel grounds on the Tuesday. The training over the first weekend was also to alternate with various bonding sessions organised by Impact Development Training Group, who were considered the leaders in this field, their other clients including such wildly disparate groups as Blue Circle Cement, Jersey International Airport, the *Daily Mail* newspaper and Manchester United Football Club. The Lions, with an obvious goal waiting ten thousand miles away and all the financial and personal motivation in the world, must have been – almost literally – a walk in the park.

This choreographed fastening together of hearts and

minds had been tried for the first time before South Africa in 1997 and it had been felt that the team spirit and absence of damaging cliques unique to that tour had owed much to firing sponges from catapults and climbing pyramids of plastic crates at the squad's Weybridge base in the week before flying out The alternative view, voiced by a number of cynical former Lions of pre-1997 vintage, was that a successful touring conglomerate must in many ways be a total fluke and all the bridge-building in the world in 2001 would not make certain of the tour party become bosom buddies with, to take one totally arbitrary example, Austin Healey.

But the problems of bringing thirty-seven different personalities geographically, temperamentally and spiritually divided are obvious and unique to the British and Irish Lions. While the Australian side consists solely of Australians with a united goal of winning for their country – minimal motivation required there – the Lions start as a team divided. The bulk of this tour squad was also, as so often in the past, dominated by the English – a country that is the old enemy in several different languages – and the players assembled at Tylney Hall had also spent a large part of the previous three months knocking lumps out of each other in that age-old tribal blood-letting known as the Six Nations Championship. This had become a campaign where the time-honoured view of 'arrogant England' had hardly been softened by a series of thumping defeats of the competition's also-rans. It was thought that much work was required to form their own corporate identity and to abolish 'them and us' complexes, particularly among the Celtic nations. These fears extended to the choice of Tylney Hall, built in 1898 but converted in the 1930s into an outrageously indulgent four-star hotel which had been picked by Lenihan from a short list of three country retreats and earned the honour mainly because the England team had not stayed there previously.

This was considered a fairly vital component in the

29

pre-tour strategy because, with eighteen Englishmen in the squad, it was important to establish a base new to all squad members; they all had to be flung into the deep end in unison.

In fact, the veteran England prop Jason Leonard had been there before the World Cup in 1991 but it was thought he was not likely to approach someone like Jason Robinson and wreck Lenihan's best-laid plans by whispering in a proprietary manner: 'I can recommend the lobster here.'

There was also some thought given to room-sharing, the management and Johnson being the only members of the party accorded single accommodation throughout the tour. This can be a delicate matter as there are players who snore, some who like to go to bed early and others addicted to late-night DVD sessions. There are chronically untidy players like Richard Hill and others who liked to hang their clothes neatly in the built-in wardrobes. It would also have been harmful, to both men, to put reformed boozer and born-again Christian Jason Robinson in with the noted larrikin Rob Henderson. Initially, the management stuck to a tried and tested formula of putting rivals for playing positions in together – Simon Taylor was Lawrence Dallaglio's 'roomy', Scott Murray was in with Jeremy Davidson to quote two examples – to demonstrate how magnanimous they could be to each other. Robinson, as it transpired, spent a lot of his tour sharing with Brian O'Driscoll, who still lived at home in Dublin with his ma and da. That seemed a fair compromise. O'Driscoll later reported that they got on like a house on fire with the proviso that 'Jason does spend rather a long time in the bathroom'. Not enough to cause a divorce, however.

In the old days of amateurism the emotional attachments of a touring team would be forged by heading into town en masse to get legless in a convenient hostelry before helping each other into a waiting taxi and sneaking into the hotel beneath a management curfew. Bonds lasting for lifetimes had been made in this way, but since the advent of professional rugby alcohol had come to be looked upon in the same murky light as bacon sandwiches, cream cakes and rest days; it was definitely off the menu, although Caffreys – not available at Tylney Hall – had won the right to be considered 'the official British Lions beer'.

Lenihan himself, when asked to put his finger on the difference between the 1989 and 2001 Lions was to admit: 'Well, we've been together three and a half days now and haven't been down to the pub yet.' It earned a big laugh in the press conference, but it was plain he was only half-joking and the smile on his face was almost wistful. This, after all, was a man noted in Australia twelve years previously for an uncanny ability to sniff out Australian pubs that sold Guinness . . .

As it transpired, on the 2001 tour, players were invariably too knackered to drink. The nearest public house from Tylney Hall was a five-mile walk away and professional sportsmen are not given to walking further than a couple of hundred yards if they can avoid it. So there was no traditional relief for players as, between some alarmingly extended training sessions, they self-consciously marched round the hotel grounds banging drums in unison, paddled dragon boats on a nearby lake or climbed shaky pyramids made up of their own team-mates. There was also a jamming session with the players forming an impromptu orchestra that featured Lawrence Dallaglio on the glockenspiel, Simon Taylor as Mr Tambourine Man and the head coach Graham Henry on the big bass drum. Lenihan, the man from Cork, declined an opportunity to perform on the flute. Some measure of the ensuing bedlam, which drove most of the parkland wildlife into hiding, can be gleaned from Henry's complaint that 'everyone was out of tune except me'.

At the evening sessions, individual Lions had to stand in front of their team-mates and list their attributes, failings as a person and goals as a player, along with a motto that they believed summed them up. And, all the while, a bunch of characters carrying klaxons and clipboards stood in the background looking earnest and encouraging.

I sneaked into Tylney Hall two days ahead of the official media day. This was simply an early effort to ingratiate myself with any Lions or management I could find and also an effort to make the world aware that no expense was being spared to keep Lions morale high and ensure ultimate success in Australia.

It would have taken a Michael Winner not to be impressed by the luxury on offer. There were sixty-five acres of immaculately kept grounds surrounding the hotel and the entrance to the grounds lay at the end of miles of lanes so leafy that the car headlights had to be switched on in broad daylight. There was a parkland golf course attached and facilities that included a croquet lawn, indoor and outdoor swimming pools and a trouser press in every room. Nearby tourist attractions included Jane Austen's house, where she wrote *Sense and Sensibility*, the Duke of Wellington's estate, Windsor Castle and Legoland. It was, in all respects, the heart of Middle England, an impression reinforced by the balmy June weather and the distant calling of peacocks in the background. Half-way up the approach road, however, stood the first reminder that for this week at least this was no ordinary establishment and that some Very Important People were in residence – an apologetic security officer armed with a list of hotel guests and a pencil to tick off names. This I took as more evidence of Lenihan's careful planning: a real fear of a fanatical raiding party from the Earls Court cell of the Wallabies Independent Supporters' Association sneaking into the grounds bent on spiking the Lions' electrolyte drinks or making off with a few key players. The uniform had plainly grasped the ridiculousness of the situation, smiling feebly at the inevitable facile joke about 'the Aussies kidnapping Martin Johnson'. More evidence of the frightening security operation came in hotel reception where a large gentleman with battered features and a uniform three sizes too small eyed arriving guests suspiciously. It turned out in later conversation that he had played rugby league for Halifax, had a large tattoo on his forearm which read 'Love, Mother' and when asked about his hotel training he winked knowingly. If he was a concierge, Graham Henry was the Lord High Druid of the Llangollen Eistedfodd.

The receptionist, who had an advanced diploma in four-star sniffiness, also proved remarkably coy about the where-abouts of the Lions. She had plainly been carefully briefed about the deviousness of the press. 'We didn't expect you lot until tomorrow,' she told me without bothering to hide her disdain. With prices ranging from £140 to £275 per room per night this seemed less than just.

As it turned out the players' accommodation was ranged around the hotel's garden wing, well away from the hoi polloi in the main hotel. They also had their own dining room and selected staff to wait on them hand and foot. I quickly set about taking advantage of the early arrival, trying hard not to look prying as I toured the gloomy corridors and lavish grounds. A look in the tiny gym revealed the bench press machine set on the highest weight – a sure sign that prop forwards were in residence – and just outside the changing room the unmistakable head of Keith Wood was bobbing up and down in the deep end of the outdoor swimming pool, the Irishman blowing like a grampus while Steve Black looked on encouragingly. It looked as though it had been a long, hard season for the hooker.

A chat with another uniform desultorily polishing the headlights of a large, luxury coach with blacked-out, one-way windows revealed that the Lions were due to train at the army rugby union ground that afternoon. He seemed quite excited that he was to drive the cream of British rugby around for a week, but unimpressed with the fact that although the coach was parked less than one hundred metres from the hotel entrance he was expected to negotiate the narrow driveway and pick them up outside the front door. I mentioned something about conserving energy. He said: 'They're big lads, aren't they? A bit on the quiet side, though.' I said something about things on their mind and being professionals. He still looked puzzled. On the way back to my room I passed a tall, shaven-headed man with a tracksuit plastered with NTL logos and carrying a camcorder. From the 'I know something you don't know' expression on his face I took him to be one of the film crew making the official Lions film. I was getting quite good at the detective work by then.

The players had met for the first time on the Saturday evening at the hotel, with an 8a.m. wake-up call on the Sunday and an official, initial get-together where Henry announced the teams for the first two matches of the tour, against Western Australia and a Queensland President's XV, and some of the less secure players departed for lunch desperately trying to read some significance into the selection. In fact, the first two matches were designed to give as many players as possible a game. Even Johnson was not named in the opening fixtures.

The first full-blown training session at Aldershot was scheduled for ninety minutes on the Monday afternoon, but in fact went on for over two hours, a scenario that was to become increasingly familiar over the next few weeks. James Robson, the doctor, began what was to be one of the longest surgeries in the history of medical practice by working out who was fit and unfit for duty the next day. Robson's attention to detail was a notable effort, considering that he had been due to move house that weekend. In the end, his gallant wife managed on her own.

By the time all thirty-seven players, with their back-up support of coaches, manager, physio, masseur, baggage man, doctor and fitness adviser climbed into their transport for the short trip to Aldershot and the army ground on Monday afternoon – pursued by various sponsors' agents in the supplied Land Rovers and one journalist in a hire car – it had been established by Robson who could train, who could not train, who could take part in the contact sessions, and who would have to sit these out.

Mike Catt, Danny Grewcock and Dai Young took no part, while of the rest, Jonny Wilkinson, Iain Balshaw and Lawrence Dallaglio were limited to non-contact situations; Balshaw and Wilkinson contented themselves with the occasional stretching and punting a ball back and forth between them. The mood was serious and business-like. Even Lenihan, although taking no active part, gamely stripped down to training top and shorts and still looked as though he could do some damage. I had never seen such massive legs – and watching rugby you do see a lot of big limbs – on a human being.

It was in this unlikely setting, with its surreal background of barracks, bored-looking squaddies, hastily erected sponsors' advertising hoardings and a handful of press and public, that the Lions began the process that would, it was hoped, culminate in a series victory against the world champions. They had eight days before the first game in Perth and that first training session crackled with urgency, but even at that early stage simple mathematics told onlookers that the number of specialist coaches plus impact sessions divided into thirty-seven players and multiplied by hours in a day would equal some lengthy sessions. Larder and Robinson wanted 50% of the working day but had to make do with 30% because Dave Alred had to work with the kickers. Steve Black wanted input, too.

Henry had divided his squad into two, with half under the control of Larder, the others in the hands of Robinson, the head man patrolling the area between the two groups in a Duke of Edinburgh-like, hands-behind-back, supervisory capacity, but with minimal input. This was the first time he had worked with specialist coaches and, like everyone else, seemed to be finding his way.

At one end of the pitch Larder ran his noted England defensive drills: these involved defenders in a strictly regimented spaced line moving in unison from side to side like the forward line in a game of table football as another line of players carrying a rugby ball probed for gaps. They were also practising what is known in the trade as 'communication,' something else imported from rugby league. League players recruited to rugby union may not in many cases have been much good, but they were all big on communication. 'What Joe/Bernard/Barry did bring to the team was communication' as the union coaches loved to say of their converts. League had always been big on talking to each other during the heat of battle. In my day you shouted things like 'Top' or 'Bottom' as the ball carrier approached to signify your intention to wrap up a pair of ankles while your team-mate attempted to take the head off. Pre-Larder, apparently, the England rugby union midfield used to stand around in total silence. That was why, as the coach quartered one half of the field with his measured, pigeon-toed stalk, his defenders babbled continuously, like a particularly heated gathering of the Trades Union Congress.

At the opposite end of the pitch Robinson's session was basically how to break down a defence organised by someone like Larder – in this case his opposite number in the Australian camp John Muggleton, another import from rugby league. Muggleton was into drift defences and communication in a big way, too, and the Wallabies had become the meanest side in the world, meaner even than England and conceded just one try throughout the entire tournament when winning the World Cup 18 months previously.

Robinson's session was called 'continuity' and involved the clearing out of bodies – in this case some anxious-looking Lions players cowering behind tackle bags – from the ball and the rucking and mauling designed to retain possession. It was a fearsome affair with players piling into each other with reckless abandon. Scott Quinnell, the massive Wales No 8, retired with a cut head and even Henry seemed concerned with Robinson's confrontational methods.

But it was an instructive tableau, demonstrating what a

simple game rugby union is when opposition and referee are removed. On one small playing field in Hampshire were the basics of the game the Lions would take to Australia, like one of those complex graphics so beloved of the quality Sunday newspapers. Balshaw and Wilkinson punting the ball back and forth completed the picture and all that was missing were a few arrows going in different directions and a headline which read: 'How the Lions will wallop the Wallabies'.

There was also an awful lot of swearing and cursing. 'Too fucking slow,' bawled Larder at frequent intervals as most of the non-English players struggled to cope with the shifting pace and alignments they were plainly unused to. Robinson was more specific: 'This,' he said, pointing to a badly abused tackle bag, 'is George Smith, the fucking Wallabies flanker. The Aussies are the best in the world at killing the ball, so ruck him out of the fucking way!' Robinson stopped short of painting the bag green and gold and planting a dreadlocked wig on its head, but the inference was obvious – the Lions feared Smith and when I related this story to him three weeks later at Coffs Harbour a few days before the First Test the player cracked a little smile of delight. As he was many judges' choice as man of the series he proved far more mobile and durable than a tackle bag.

After the elongated training session the small group of journalists present were granted an impromptu first audience with Lenihan and Henry. I knew my place and hid at the back as the most high-profile rugby writers in Britain fixed the manager and coach with beady eyes and began the questioning that was to go on for the next two months. This was obviously less an attempt to prise a story out of them and more an attempt to establish some sort of pecking order. They were saying to Lenihan and Henry in effect: 'Remember my face. You will have to give serious answers to my serious questions in the weeks ahead!'

But Henry dutifully revealed that he was determined to

repay all the faith shown in him and that he was ahead of schedule in terms of where he wanted to be with his squad while Lenihan, after outlining the state of the injured – a piece of business that was to be repeated on a daily basis in the weeks ahead – did reveal that the Lions had lost one important battle against Australia already, claiming that they had reneged on an agreement to have neutral referees in the build-up games.

'Our understanding was that the refs would be neutral in seven games, including the three Tests,' said Lenihan. 'I am annoyed that is not the case and will be looking to resolve it.' In the end, he never did and the Lions were lumbered by some of the worst officaldom ever seen on a rugby field for some of the non-Test games.

Tuesday had been the day that the majority of players were least looking forward to as the world's media descended on Tylney Hall to discover the hopes, fears and ambitions of the assembled Lions.

'I think I'll have to drop out with a sore throat,' said Martin Johnson – never previously known for his fondness of journalists – in an aside to the press lining the side of the pitch at Aldershot the day before. After two days of hard work with Larder and Robinson, however, some of the players were already feeling the strain and the media session arrived as a blessed relief.

From my hotel window I watched with pouting dismay as the rest of the press arrived en masse. For two days it had been, gloriously, the Lions plus me – although of course they had not been aware of that fact. I felt like the little boy who spends half a day building a sandcastle on the beach only for a bunch of bigger boys to appear and trample all over it.

There had been half a dozen rugby writers on the Monday at Aldershot but now the bodies bearing cameras, notebooks and microphones were expanding amoebae-like into something vast and uncontrollable. Six weeks later, by the time of the deciding Test, the media outnumbered the official Lions party by two to one and in the week before the series decider there were more Scottish pressmen than Scottish players.

As I had been there first at least I could adopt the casual, proprietary air of one who knows his way around and I soon slipped into the habits of the rugby press. This invariably consisted of presenting opinion as incontrovertible fact, slagging off Henry and name-dropping – usually players' nicknames – like schoolboys. Thus, in the same conversation we could have a writer saying: 'Hendo (Rob Henderson) will play inside centre in the Tests' and 'Daws (Matt Dawson) tells me he is knackered already.' One journalist mysteriously referred constantly to someone called 'Rog' while the rest of us racked our brains trying to work out who he meant. There was no player called Roger so it must have been someone from the sponsors, until he started going on about goal-kicking and it became clear he was talking about Ronan O'Gara. The journalist in question, naturally, had never met O'Gara in his life.

I soon got into the swing of things.

'I was talking to Johnno today.' Casual.

'And?' Sceptical.

'He is very focused.' (I had indeed spoken to Johnson that day, wishing him good morning on the way to the dining room; he had ignored me.)

Alex Broun appeared with the official media guide (author A. Broun) which included a message of welcome from Lenihan, some extended warnings about the copyright of sponsors' logos and sundry statistics about previous Lions tours, match venues and heights and weights of players. The sort of useless data, in fact, that no journalist could afford to be without.

The booklet earned eight out of ten for content but lost out a little on facts, particularly the generous translation of kilograms into pounds (Neil Jenkins was listed at 13st 7lb and 102kg) and some dubious misspellings ('person I would most like to meet: Mahammad Ali'). Apart from that, it offered a revealing anthropological guide into what makes rugby players tick, but which some of them should perhaps have kept to themselves. The Irish lock, Malcolm O'Kelly, for example, promised some alarming dressing-room rituals and, asked to describe his pre-match preparations, he nominated 'young virginal sacrificing'. It was also alarming to learn that our great hope Brian O'Driscoll's favourite film was *Dumb and Dumber*. Jason Leonard's wish to meet Babe Ruth and Rocky Marciano looked likely to remain unrequited in his present life-time, and for players to describe themselves constantly as 'easy-going' did seem a non-sequitur, given their chosen profession. There was also welcome evidence of a sense of humour behind the fearsome countenance of our leader. Asked to describe himself, Martin Johnson wrote 'very dull'; the thing he could least do without was 'oxygen' and pre-match preparation involved 'getting changed into my rugby kit'.

The working area for the media was laid out on one of the manicured back lawns of Tylney Hall where thirty or so parasols and plastic tables and chairs were waiting in the glare of the afternoon sun. There were patio doors leading into a lounge and stone balustrades everywhere and the surroundings were *Brideshead*-like. If Charles Ryder and Sebastian Flyte had bounced into view in their tennis gear no one would have batted an eyelid. Like making a doctor's appointment, journalists had to approach Broun and nominate a tourist for interview. One chair was for a player/coach while on the other side were three or more seats for his interrogators.

It was like a vast, aristocratic garden party with micro-phones and notebooks in place of the canapés and cucumber sandwiches. Talk was confined exclusively to the tour and it proved an illuminating initial insight into the Lions. For the old soldiers in the party, days like these were like shelling peas and players such as Dallaglio and Leonard reeled off interview after interview without breaking sweat.

At one point Dallaglio picked up a tape recorder from

the table in front of him and studied it with a curious half-smile, maybe thinking back to the infamous *News of the World* tapes two years previously that had cost him the England captaincy, and almost his career. He sounded less than upbeat about the tour and his role in it. A radio reporter asked him 'how the leg was?' and Dallaglio, in his characteristic, Italianate fashion, shrugged his shoulders, raised his hands and said: 'It's OK.' Five minutes later another journalist asked him the identical question and Dallaglio, instead of expressing surprise that anyone could be so dim, gave the identical reaction and reply. He seemed almost fatalistic.

Tom Smith's recent revelation that he had to cope with epilepsy made him an obvious, if reluctant, target, while most of the film cameras dwelt almost exclusively on the boyish, photogenic features of England's stand-off, young Wilkinson. An interview with Wilkinson was a remarkable affair. I had never witnessed anyone yawn as much – massive, noisy, cavernous whale-like yawns – and say so little. Whether this was his nature, or whether he had schooled himself to be deliberately unforthcoming remained unclear.

Journalists queued to ask Matt Dawson the same annoying question about 1997 and how an injury to Rob Howley gave him a Test place and Henry probably had to answer the same question about the tradition of the Lions a hundred times. Rob Henderson, a throwback to the days of amateurism with his fondness for a pint and a Marlboro Lite, was also a popular interviewee with journalists who could equate with such things. Jason Robinson, since his days in rugby league, seemed to have perfected an unblinking, unsmiling, oddly disconcerting stare for interrogators.

The Scottish press contingent had conspiratorially arranged to interview their small representation of players in a group of three, based mainly on the unspoken fear that one or another would get an 'exclusive' that the others might miss, but also on the premise that as Tom Smith was not a noted extrovert, Simon Taylor supposedly a shy and stuttering

41

tour rookie and Scott Murray obsessed solely by his girl-friend and DVD players, they would be more effusive in the company of their countrymen. As it turned out, Smith surprised us all with his comparative loquacity after earning a reputation on the 1997 tour of a man not only of few words but of no words at all. He even offered us coffee – the first time I could ever recall a professional sportsman displaying such generosity. Keith Wood, his front-row colleague, was later to put all this down to 'the love of a good woman'.

Murray was quite happy to discuss the gruelling training, his rivals for the lock position and the influence of Martin Johnson without once mentioning his divine 'missus' while Taylor, with his undamaged blond good looks and air of mannered reserve looked totally at home. The party's youngest member, at 21, turned out to be less than over-awed about his circumstances and surroundings, possibly because as a law student he has a life outside rugby. He also had a self-mocking intelligence and revealed that he had been sharing with Dallaglio who seemed 'a nice guy' but also wondered jestingly 'how come Lawrence got the double bed?' Taylor's tour-ending injury a week later in Perth was a blow not only to the Scottish press who saw their interviewing opportunities cut by a third overnight but to the tourists as a whole. In particular Jonny Wilkinson who was forced to revert to his customary, unwanted role as 'baby of the party'.

There was also another reminder that Lions tours are less about rugby and more about commerce with a stage-managed presentation to Henry of his first autograph book by the young daughter of the collector who had acquired it in New Zealand in 1996. The book apparently contained signatures of sporting gods including Richie Benaud and Everton Weekes and Henry had exchanged it, as kids do, for a pair of wicket keeper's gloves. Henry was suitably moved, but did not get to keep it: the book went up for sale as the lead item on the collector's website which was opportunely launched that very day.

After the interview with the Scots en masse the search began for more prey and gazing down from the terrace on to the clustered lawn only two tourists seemed unoccupied. Will Greenwood was reading a magazine and Phil Larder was seated twiddling his thumbs, alone. Coming from the same part of North Manchester and with a rugby league background, I thought he would welcome some company and tittle tattle.

The rules for interviewing sports personalities are simple: always find some common ground before getting down to business. It should have been simple. Once, in my capacity as rugby league writer on a newspaper in Barrow-in-Furness – the Cumbria town famous only for Emlyn Hughes, the Trident nuclear submarine and the great former Great Britain rugby league captain Willie Horne – I had spoken to Larder on the telephone in his capacity as coach of the Great Britain rugby league side, also known confusingly as the British Lions (at least the Australians differentiate by calling one the Wallabies and the other the Kangaroos). Naturally, I reminded Larder of this.

'Barrow eh? How's Willie Horne these days?'

'I'm afraid Willie died a few weeks ago.'

That seemed to end the bonding session, so it was down to work. Larder, as did everyone else in this sun-drenched, idyllic opening to the tour, made all the right noises about the task ahead and the quality of the selected players – 'England are impressive, but this lot are the absolute cream' – but he did add a couple of illuminating asides. He 'could have done with more time' and when asked about his low profile with England – I could not recall an interview with him on TV or in print – he said: 'That's the way Clive (Woodward) wanted to run things.'

Woodward had also apparently expressed some concern when Larder was appointed to the Lions job that the rest of the 'Celts' might pick up on England's defensive strategies in time for the next Six Nations. Larder also proved remarkably prescient when he said: 'We've got only six matches

43

up to the First Test and no settled side to work with. The crucial thing is to make sure that we're all singing from the same hymn sheet. Just one thing out of kilter and the whole show can come apart.'

In fact, by midday on Friday June 1 when the Lions of 2001 walked through a large throng of cheering fans at Heathrow Airport to board Singapore Airlines flight SQ317 for the 22-hour flight to the other side of the earth where the world champions were waiting, there were already a few things out of kilter. Some players were muttering about the harshness of the training – particularly the Andy Robinson sessions – and the perceived lack of communication between themselves and management. And Henry's remark on the first day at Aldershot that 'Robbo's going at it so hard I thought he might leave some of them behind' was also about to come back and haunt him.

BAD BLOOD

'I hope you come a bloody good second.' They were the first words that I heard from an Australian on Australian soil and they came from a middle-aged customs officer at Brisbane Airport as he snapped my passport shut. It had taken all of five minutes – the time between collecting my baggage and going through immigration – to realise that when Donald Horne, author of *The Lucky Country* wrote: 'Sport to many Australians is life and the rest a shadow', he had not been far wrong. I asked the customs officer if he was a rugby fan. He preferred 'footie' – Australian Rules Football – but then added, with what can best be described as cheerful menace: 'I can remember 1989, though.' Over the next few weeks it was to become clear that he was not the only Australian with a long memory.

The recollection of the rumbustious 1989 tour of Australia by the British Lions hung over its 2001 counterpart like an angry black cloud. Conversations with Australian rugby journalists, players, coaches and fans were dominated by '89 and twelve years later still simmered with the unforgiving rancour of an ancient feud.

The wounds from that tour had been left unstitched and had been festering ever since and they were to plague the 2001 manager Donal Lenihan. Try as he might to insist that it was useless to rake over the ashes of incidents that many of the current players could scarcely remember, it still cropped up, always with the insinuation that the 2001 tourists would copy their counterparts of twelve years previously. Lenihan made one impassioned plea early on in the tour to let bygones be bygones, saying after the Queensland match: 'There seems to be a hangover from 1989. Every time you pick up a paper you read about 1989, and every time you open a rugby magazine you see pictures of incidents from

45

then, but that's all in the past and it's a totally different game now. I wish people would just close the book on it and let it go. We're here to play rugby, and that's it.'

After that he simply refused to comment. This was looked on as even more inflammatory.

After the New South Wales Waratahs match on the fourth Saturday of the tour, a game which had all the gruesome fascination of a bare-knuckle prize fight but with none of its skills, Lenihan was asked by an Australian journalist, Jeff Wells of the *Daily Telegraph*: 'Is there anything you would like to say to the Wallabies or anybody else to prevent a bloodbath in the First Test?' Lenihan, still coming to terms with a game that had seen a blood-curdling assault on the Lions fly-half Ronan O'Gara, a sending-off and five yellow cards, quite reasonably said no. This was immediately construed as an official declaration of war. Wells, the sort of one-eyed, in-your-face sports columnist considered essential to the back pages of every Australian newspaper, proceeded to write on the Thursday before the First Test: 'Very well, Mr Lenihan, let the troubles resume. The spirit of '89 lives! It's an eye for an eye, a stomp for a stomp.' He concluded by saying: 'The peace pipe stays in the locker.'

Little wonder that when the Lions captain of 1989, Finlay Calder, met his 2001 counterpart in Sydney he told Martin Johnson, only half-jokingly: 'I think I should apologise for 1989!'

When the Lions arrived that year they found Wallaby rugby in a healthy state. Five years previously they had toured the British Isles, beating all four home nations with sumptuous displays of attacking rugby, and in 1987 they had co-hosted, with New Zealand, the first World Cup, beating England early on and eventually losing an epic semi-final against France, and Serge Blanco, in Sydney. In 1989 they boasted players of the calibre of Michael Lynagh, Nick Farr-Jones and David Campese in the backs and a pack only slightly less able. In a land which worshipped almost exclusively the rugby league Kangaroos and their cricketers, union had finally found a toehold in public esteem. Beating the Lions would reinforce their credibility and their new popularity.

The '89 tour was also the first in a hundred years to tour Australia exclusively, unlike previous visits when a couple of games there were looked on as a gentle warm-up en route to the real thing in New Zealand. This had done little to help basic Australian insecurities and, like many other things from the old country, the Lions would be something Australia could measure themselves against. To put it mildly, it became important to win the series.

On the promotional front the Lions did their bit in 1989, touring the outposts to spread the gospel. In the first game in Perth they beat Western Australia 44–0 and Australia B 23–18 in Melbourne. The complexion of the tour changed dramatically, however, in Brisbane when they lined up against Queensland. Mike Hall, the Welsh centre, was badly raked while lying on the ground and the Lions retaliated. Mark McBain, the Queensland hooker, had been warned by his opposite number, Brian Moore, about his habit of collapsing scrums and, when he persisted, one of the Lions locks hammered the message home with a fist. Bill Campbell, the Wallabies' Test lock, claimed he had been punched at virtually every line-out and at the after-match function gave what amounted to an implicit warning that the Wallabies would meet fire with fire in the First Test in Sydney. His complaints were given huge coverage in the Australian media; the Lions were playing 'Thugby', not rugby and were the dirtiest bunch to set foot on Australian soil since the first convicts.

The home press also had a field day after the Lions lost the First Test conclusively and the same journalists who had savaged the tourists on TV and in newspapers for strong-arm tactics after the Queensland game now questioned their manhood. It was all the motivation the Lions needed and as Calder has also pointed out so many times since: 'We knew we had three weeks in Australia after the Second Test. The thought of spending all that time there after losing the series was horrendous. If that wasn't enough, when we arrived at Ballymore the crowd were yelling things like: "Here come the Lions. More like pussy cats. Miaow!" So what did they expect?'

The Battle of Ballymore, or rather *one* of the Battles of Ballymore, began with a preliminary scuffle involving the two scrum-halfs, Robert Jones of the Lions and the Wallabies' captain Nick Farr-Jones and the game was disfigured from then on by a number of brawls, most of them won conclusively by the Lions. In between the fist fights the Wallabies pack were being pulverised. The Lions won the Test 19–12 and went on to take the series in Sydney, thanks to an extraordinary late gaffe by Campese. But what hurt the Australians more than losing the series was losing the fight, particularly as some of the home forwards had been posted missing in the heat of battle. They had been out-machoed, an unforgivable state of affairs for an Australian sportsman, and the whingeing began. They were still whingeing twelve years later, their state of mind not helped in the interim by jocular after-dinner speeches by the likes of Moore who gleeefully described the 1989 Lions Test pack at Ballymore who contained Police Constables Wade Dooley and Dean Richards along with Chief Inspector Paul Ackford taking part in 'the most legal fight in the history of rugby'.

As with many other sporting matters the Australian memory tends to be selective. The 1989 incidents in Brisbane, in fact, paled into significance alongside the first Battle of Ballymore 14 years earlier when England had played the Wallabies there. That match had seen an extraordinary start when, after Australia kicked off, the home forwards flew into their opposite numbers like guests on the *Jerry Springer Show*. The assault, led by the long-haired flanker Ray Price and the hooker Peter Horton, was so obviously premeditated as to be almost comical although the referee, an Australian, claimed he had seen nothing that merited even a reprimand.

Price, on the strength of his heroics that day, later picked up a rugby league contract and it could have been a lot worse for England. The young Australian prop Steve Finnane was missing for the Second Test but had already made his mark in earlier matches by knocking cold the England lock Bill Beaumont and prop Mike Burton and earning an immediate niche as one of sport's great intimidators, a Norman Hunter or Dick Butkus of his profession. Finnane was unusual in that he was a skilled pugilist, unlike most rugby forwards who are almost unanimously chronically bad performers at the Noble Art. He was also sneaky with it and 26 years later the memory of the 'Phantom Puncher' still occasioned a wince or two from the England full-back of that day, Radio Five commentator Alastair Hignell.

The Ballymore Test ended in overwhelming defeat for England and also saw the sending-off of Burton – later to become the corporate king of Twickenham – in the first act of retaliation, so the Australians were given the opportunity to win the propaganda war, too. That 1975 assault by the Wallabies forwards, however, seemed conveniently to slip minds when the words 'Battle' and 'Ballymore' came up in conversation and for those Australian fans and journalists who still believed that not a single act of foul play had ever been perpetrated by a Wallaby in the game's history, the evidence was clad in green and gold and staring them in the face when the 2001 series began. Flanker Owen Finegan was just getting over a suspension for stamping on his Australia team-mate Michael Foley while the No 8 Toutai Kefu was still best remembered by British journalists for his stand-up fight with the Irish forward Trevor Brennan during a World Cup tie in 1999.

Under the constant battering over the head with 1989, the British media of 2001 also did their best to retaliate. This took the time-honoured form of lobbing traditional national stereotypes back and forth like hand grenades; the Australians were ex-convicts, crude, uncultured, and foul-mouthed and we were quick to pick up on the case of John Hopoate, the Northern Eagles rugby league player who was just finishing a lengthy ban for poking his fingers up the bums of opponents in the tackle. He seemed to us the quintessential Australian sportsman.

To Australian journalists the Lions were imperious, arrogant and ruthless and would almost certainly carry on where their '89 cousins had left off, given half the chance. This was what they wanted to believe and nothing was going to deter them from that mindset. After one sustained rant in print against the Lions which again invoked 1989 I invited the Australian author of the piece to meet Calder, on the basis that there are two sides to every argument. Calder, for example, had spent twelve years claiming that the Lions of '89 simply employed fierce commitment, rather than naked violence. This was not what Australia wanted to hear and the journalist discovered he had other things to do.

Many of the current Australian players, of course, were still in short pants in 1989, but whether they liked it or not there were constant reminders from a small army of ex-players and coaches with the long memory of a *mafiosi*. Mark McBain, yes that Mark McBain, was now coaching Queensland and Bob Dwyer, the Australia coach in 1989, was in charge of New South Wales. If their constant carping were not enough, some of the Australian combatants of 1989, notably Farr-Jones, Campese and Simon Poidevin, were happy to stir the pot.

There were other reminders around. Dai Young, who had stood on the head of the Wallaby lock Steve Cutler at Ballymore, was in the 2001 tour party and Lenihan and Andy Robinson had also toured in 1989. A large chunk of the '89 squad were also in Australia in various promotional capacities and they included Calder, Ieuan Evans, Gareth Chilcott and Jerry Guscott. Rob Andrew and Paul Ackford were part of the press crew which caused a few hilarious moments, particularly when the big screen at Test matches would show a replay of Ballymore – and Ackford wading into the Australian pack to encouraging cries of 'Go on Ackers!' from colleagues.

The positive side of all this muck-raking was that it did sell tickets because interest in the Lions was not exactly overwhelming. There were no queues of Australian school-boy autograph hunters outside their hotels and most of the tourists went unrecognised in the street. The home sports pages were dominated by league and 'footie' and even soccer, because Australia were in the throes of qualify-ing for the World Cup at the time. There was far more media and public interest in the forthcoming Tri Nations series, the self-styled unofficial world championship featur-ing Australia, New Zealand and South Africa played on a home and away basis and, for the modern Wallaby rugby fan still basking in the after-glow of a World Cup, Tri Nations and Bledisloe Cup wins there wasn't much to get excited about in a scratch touring team whose last appearance had been in a different lifetime. Nor did beating the Lions have quite the same kudos for Australia as a triumph over the All Blacks or the Springboks. Everyone Down Under did recognise one thing, however: the Lions of 2001 offered a golden opportunity for Australia to settle a few old scores.

The campaign began as soon as the Lions touched down with Dwyer and the ACT Brumbies coach Eddie Jones launch-ing a propaganda offensive against the tourists so well timed and co-ordinated that it had to be pre-planned. They complained about the Lions' scrummaging, their line-out tactics, ball-killing at the ruck and of course their violence, only desisting when the Lions went one up in the series without throwing a single punch. After that, 1989, oddly, was mentioned only in the context of pointing out that Australia would now have to emulate those Lions and over-turn a 1–0 deficit. It was almost inevitable, however, that somewhere between touching down in Perth and arriving in Brisbane for the First Test all the bad blood would spill over into open warfare.

Until the third week and the start of the real hostilities the tour had progressed in the manner of twelve years previously with trips to the outback to spread the gospel. There was a fixture against Western Australia in Perth, another soft game – on paper at least – against a Queensland President's XV in Townsville and finally the real meat, Saturday games against the Super 12 sides Queensland and New South Wales, sandwiching a Tuesday fixture against Australia A.

The Lions certainly started with a swagger and the game against Western Australia at the vast cricket oval of the WACA, on Friday June 8, produced a record 116–10 win and three tries apiece for wing Dan Luger and the No 8 Scott Quinnell. There were also two tries each for Rob Howley, Neil Back and Iain Balshaw, with Simon Taylor, Mark Taylor, Will Greenwood, Austin Healey, Brian O'Driscoll and Danny Grewcock also touching down. Stand-off Ronan O'Gara kicked 26 points, completing a rout which eclipsed the 1974 Lions' record 97–0 success against South Western Districts in South Africa. It left Western Australia's former Saracens fly-half, Duncan McRae, (of whom more later) to reflect: 'They showed some great running rugby, which the northern hemisphere is not renowned for, and it looks all set up for a superb Test series. I thought the Lions were outstanding; they couldn't really have done any more. In terms of starting a tour, you would have to say it was awesome.' There were murmurings among the British media about this being possibly the greatest Lions side in history. The Western Australia captain Trefor Thomas was perhaps more accurate when he said: 'We did our best, but it was taking two or three tacklers to stop one of their players and the speed of the game was just too fast for us. We are amateurs, after all.'

Henry also donned his headmaster's hat to award the Lions '6 out of 10', adding: 'We didn't expect to be perfect without having a game together. We may not be perfect for some time. We have got to be patient, just work on our game, and I am sure the players will be dying to do that. But we have got a start now, something to build on, and that is very important.'

But there were some negative aspects. The Irish centre Brian O'Driscoll had been selected at full-back, the first little dent in the fragile confidence of the touted Test No 15 Iain Balshaw, and the two tries conceded and ten points were also a record score for Western Australia against the Lions. That did not go down too well with the defensive coach Phil Larder and the training intensified; so did Andy Robinson's growling.

The Lions had also lost their first players to injury. Simon Taylor damaged a knee ligament in the last few minutes at the WACA and Phil Greening twisted a knee in training when two of his team-mates careered into him two days before the opening match. This was to rule him out of the playing side of the tour, although like many others he hung around in a sort of semi-detached way for the rest of the trip. presumably in the hope that he would recover. In the end he nearly did, then he didn't and finally he gave up altogether and took a temporary courier's job with the travel company, Gullivers. He'd come all that way and never got to wear a Lions jersey.

There were some near misses, too. Neil Jenkins needed ten stitches after a clash of heads with Jeremy Davidson and Jason Robinson suffered an ankle knock. There was also early evidence of the Lions paranoia which was to dog the rest of the tour when a group of curious children were spotted watching training and there were mutterings from the management about spies in the camp, the eight-year-olds presumably producing detailed dossiers on the Lions' line-out tactics in their school exercise books. Journalists were also banned from much of the training and relations between the press and management declined rapidly from then on.

The injury to Taylor and the way that news broke hardly helped. Taylor, who had come on at half-time for Richard

Hill at the WACA, had made a memorable Lions debut, scoring one try and making a number of the trademark surging runs that had first caught the eye of Lenihan at Northampton. The tartan-clad media immediately began to fantasise about the Edinburgh player keeping Dallaglio out of the Test side. Taylor, however, had felt a bang on his knee twenty minutes from time and in the team hotel later he felt some discomfort there. At 11.30p.m. he went to have it checked by James Robson and twelve hours and an MRI scan later he was on his way home in tears. Taylor stayed in Perth on the Saturday night, intending to catch a Sunday flight while the rest of the squad flew on to Townsville; or rather didn't fly on to Townsville as the flight was delayed for several hours, leaving the press incommunicado as Taylor began packing and the management organised a replacement.

Over in Canada, meanwhile, where England were on their summer tour and preparing for the Second Test in Vancouver, their manager Clive Woodward was moaning about having to lose his vice-captain Martin Corry 'as a replacement for Simon Taylor'. The announcement that Taylor's tour was over came, in effect, from Woodward and the combination of circumstances – Woodward's indiscretion, the delayed flight and Lenihan's announcement of a clean bill of health for the party after the game – all added up to what the travelling media saw as outright deception.

It was an unfortunate opening to the tour, although spirits among the tiny Scottish press contingent, at an all-time low after the departure of Taylor, rose slightly with the news that Greening's replacement would be the Glasgow hooker Gordon Bulloch. The replacements were already winging in like Spanish holiday packages; the training pace did not slacken.

The game against Queensland President's XV was to take place in Dairy Farmers Stadium, home of rugby league's North Queensland Cowboys, and as a preliminary there was a long Lions team run in very humid temperatures the day before. The selected side had two full-contact sessions.

The President's men did not roll over to have their tummies tickled, either.

They were duly beaten 83–6, but it was 10–6 at half-time and there was a lot of shouting and screaming from Henry and Robinson in the interval which seemed to have an effect as the Lions came out a different team. A try after 30 seconds into the second half changed the complexion of the match instantly and a hat-trick by Jason Robinson within 17 minutes turned it into a rout. Robinson added two more tries in the final minutes and it was plain that here was the man of the moment. Already there were two teams taking shape. Jonny Wilkinson was still under wraps, but even though he hadn't played it seemed unlikely that Neil Jenkins would dislodge him, particularly after the Welshman's display at Townsville. Scrum-half Matt Dawson had also done very little to enhance his Test claims and although Colin Charvis was named man of the match and Corry, less than twenty-four hours after arriving, played the full eighty minutes, the Test back row of Scott Quinnell, Richard Hill and Neil Back was already picking itself in the minds of most journalists.

With Catt still struggling, the inside centre place – O'Driscoll was a certainty at 13 – was between Will Greenwood and Rob Henderson with the Irishman doing his chances no harm with the try of the game in Townsville, following up his own chip ahead, and adroitly gathering to cross between the posts. Such subtlety was thought to be beyond him, but he finished the game with a hat-trick.

On the downside, hooker Robin McBryde went off after only seven minutes with a bruised leg. It was turning into a bad tour for hookers.

On the Thursday following our arrival in Brisbane the press had been invited down to Ballymore to watch Queensland train. In fact the players did only 'spotting' (rehearsal of match moves at walking pace) but they all seemed remarkably relaxed and there were plenty of interview opportunities. I asked McBain about 1989 (it was becoming a habit) and he grimaced. Could he recall who his opposite number was? 'Look, mate, I don't want to bring all that up again.' He must have been the only man in Australia who didn't at that time. Former Wallabies Tim Horan and Pat Howard, who had spent the previous season playing in England's Zurich Premiership or the Zurich Superannuation Premiership as Australians call it, were at the pitch side and were duly asked for their views. Both were very diplomatic, but also managed to give the impression that there was no way the Lions would win the series.

Queensland were going into the Lions match without their captain John Eales, but he was at training and looked as fit as a flea and McBain had also pulled the expected Test full-back Chris Latham and Wallabies wing Ben Tune. Suspicious minds were activated. It did occur to some that in the light of the ease of the itinerary to date – massive victories over average opposition were considered poor preparation for the real thing – the tourists were being led up a fragrantly scented garden path with all the nasties hiding in the undergrowth and ready to spring out of ambush come the first Test in a fortnight's time.

As it turned out, although Queensland did come out fighting in an effort to prove that Ballymore was still the Madison Square Garden of rugby grounds, they were also comprehensively taken apart by the Lions. The game saw the return to action of Wilkinson, which was reassuring, but nothing was more cheering than the sight of Johnson's high-speed shuffle out ahead of his troops, Lions mascot in hand.

Even in the sang-froid-coated press box, it was difficult not to shout hurrah, such was the uplifting sight of that fearsome, frowning countenance. The supporting cast plainly saw things the same way for the Lions were inspired, running in five tries against a side who had finished fourth in the Super 12 and were expected, if not to lower the red colours, at least to give them a useful work-out.

The game was as good as over by half-time with the visitors leading 32–3 and Queensland close to total disarray. With three games gone, a 100% success rate, 241 points for and just 24 against, it was probably unreasonable to carp, but there were still a few niggling doubts. In the second half the Lions subsided into something close to incompetence with spilled ball, turnovers and a succession of penalties against. They also conceded a daft try.

Before they left Britain, too, it had always been assumed that the tourists would take every Australia side apart in the forwards, but both likely test props, Tom Smith and Phil Vickery, struggled against the Wallaby front row of Glenn Panoho and Nic Stiles and the Lions pack were shunted off their own ball with alarming ease at times. On the plus side, the Irish centre partnership of O'Driscoll and Henderson looked the real thing, with O'Driscoll posing Australia's Daniel Herbert problems he was never to resolve throughout the series. The Lions' line-out, too, functioned smoothly with Johnson and Danny Grewcock in charge and the back row of Richard Hill, Neil Back and the man who had overnight become the squad's dark horse, Martin Corry, obliterated their opposite numbers, including the likely Test No 8 Kefu. Rob Howley, although he had a knock to the ribs which forced his replacement, by the unimpressive Dawson, looked a Test certainty. All very reassuring.

Like everyone else in Australia, Queensland had obviously been examining their history books and the game erupted into a punch-up among the forwards almost from the kick-off, with Grewcock – a black belt at judo as the Australian newspapers never ceased to remind us – and Hill and the home hooker Michael Foley heavily involved. When Vickery then retaliated for a raking of the wing, Dafydd James, while the Welshman was trapped on the wrong side of a ruck, there had been more whistle and talk from referee Stuart Dickinson than meaningful action. It was almost a relief when the home stand-off, Elton Flatley, put the first points on the board with a penalty. The home side stayed on the offensive when Herbert kicked into space, full-back Michael Tabrett took play on and winger David McCallum (nicknamed, inevitably, Kuriaykin) was forced into touch by James.

Three minutes later, Queensland were turned over in midfield, and the Lions were away with Wood, Wilkinson, James and Howley scampering into home territory. When play broke down, Back's long pass found Wilkinson who, looking up and spotting a flat and converging home defence, kicked high for Dan Luger to gather and go in at the corner. A marvellously unexpected deft kick from Henderson took play back into the Queensland 22, and when Tabrett messed up his clearance, Queensland collapsed the five-yard scrum and Wilkinson kicked the Lions' first penalty of the tour.

The tourists went further ahead when Corry charged down a kick by Flatley and Hill bobbled the ball on for Henderson to seize gratefully and cross. A Wilkinson penalty made it 18–3 for the Lions, and more evidence that they could do little wrong came when, after Corry smashed the Queensland lock Nathan Sharp in midfield to earn possession, Wood took the pass from Smith, and chipped over the defence for James to gather without breaking his stride. Wilkinson's superb inside pass then put Hill over and the stand-off's conversion made it 32–3 at half-time.

But then, suddenly, all the momentum vanished. Although O'Driscoll slipped through for a try within five minutes of the re-start, Queensland finally found the fighting spirit of their ancestors and the Lions were suddenly being harried into error, not helped by an evening dew, a slippery ball, an insistence on running kickable penalties, and Howley's replacement by Dawson. Another Wilkinson penalty took the score past the 40-mark, but on seventy minutes Queensland scrum-half Sam Cordingley charged down Dawson's painfully slow clearance and touched down for only the third try against the tourists in three matches. Still three too many for Phil Larder, of course.

The after-match press conference was enlivened by a pair

of Australian 'journalists' who had plainly been sampling the sponsors' products and were very much the worse for wear. It turned out they were two punters who had bet each other that they could get into a Lions press conference. One of them even asked Johnson something on the lines of: 'How important was victory tonight?' He had obviously done his homework and even knew the correct calibre of daft questions.

The Queensland captain Daniel Herbert also demonstrated the art of being graciously dismissive when discussing the Lions, saying: 'I still believe nothing is beyond the Australia side; we have proved that time and time again over the last few years. We can win under any circumstances. I don't think that [our coach] Rod Macqueen will have learned anything new, either from tonight.'

He also said, somewhat enigmatically: 'I would say the Lions are the best side the Wallabies will have faced in the last twelve months.'

McBain, their coach, also refused to be overwhelmed, asking somewhat uncharitably: 'They seem to have a Plan A, but do they have a Plan B?' He also managed to label the Lions – 31 tries in three matches – 'boring' because of their insistence on using the rolling maul. It was hard to please some people.

Wilkinson showed no ill-effects after his recent neck injury and his eight weeks off seemed to have done him no harm at all. As Graham Henry put it in his quaint way: 'Jonny navigated the ship well.' We soon recognised this as one of Henry's favourite sayings, as was 'the top three inches (of the head) are the most important in this game' and 'he is holding his hand up for selection'. Asked about the performance of Corry, Henry said: 'I think he is telling the Lions' selectors they made a mistake not picking him in the first place. He is holding his hand up for a Test place in no uncertain manner.' Corry, who arrived at the press conference with the rabid, eyes-dilated look of a performer in a Bruce Lee movie, was to hold up his hand a lot.

The day after the Ballymore game the tour party took the short flight to Sydney and what was to become our second home in Australia, the Manly Pacific Hotel. The clever old hands among the journalists had taken the precaution of telephoning ahead to ensure they got seafront rooms; the remainder of us had to be content with views across the Manly suburbs, the positive aspect of this being that with the aid of binoculars I could watch the Lions training at Manly Oval, home of the resort's rugby union club, some 400 yards away. Manly is a rugby league town, once home to one of the great clubs of Australian history and a team that had once boasted at different times, Bobby Fulton, Malcolm Reilly and Steve Norton. Reilly, the former Great Britain coach (Larder was his assistant) had stayed in the Manly Pacific 30 years previously when he arrived from Castleford and it hadn't changed much since with an infuriatingly slow elevator, uninspiring bedrooms and appalling bar service.

Manly itself was a strange mix. There were heart-breakingly beautiful girls in bikinis playing beach volleyball or power-walking along the promenade and drunken Islanders staggering round the streets at night. Surly Maoris manned the doors of most of the pubs. No one, girls or drunks, batted an eyelid at the arrival of one of sport's great touring sides and the Lions were free to look around unmolested, many of them wandering round at night with the puzzled aimlessness of package tourists on their first trip abroad.

Braced by the sunshine and sea air, the press experienced a collective rush of blood to heads with a mass jog on the first evening, the numbers diminishing rapidly in the days ahead. Some of us joined a local gym, run by a school mate of George Smith and where a New Zealander named Don frightened us with tales of his work as an assistant to the former Wallabies conditioning coach Steve Nance. Apparently one of their sessions involved sprints of ten times two hundred metres in under thirty-five seconds with two minutes rest in between. Their best performer at this was the 110kg hooker, Phil Kearns.

Over the couple of days leading up to the game against Australia A in Gosford there was more evidence that Australia wanted to win this series rather badly. Eddie Jones, the coach of both the Super 12 champions Brumbies and the national A side as well as Rod Macqueen's nominated successor, produced another stinging attack on the tourists and their alleged aggressive style of play. These opinions came, not in a newspaper, but an official press release from the Australian Rugby Union, who were quite happy to circulate Jones's opinions with little regard for the fact that it was not exactly the height of hospitality. After the happy, back-slapping welcome the hosts were now twisting the knife in the back. Jones also called on New Zealand referee Paul Honiss, due to take charge of the A team game, to keep an eye on the Lions 'bully boys'. He concluded with the pious hope that 'commonsense would prevail', another classic Australianism.

Nothing ever felt right about the night of the Australia A match. It took an hour and a half in a bizarre rush hour – bizarre because we seemed to be in the middle of nowhere – to get to Gosford, with night falling soon after we set off. The last half-hour was spent driving in total darkness until the North Power Stadium lit up the wilderness in a strangely menacing way, like the alien-spotting compound in *Close Encounters*. The long drive and the unearthly surroundings had plainly upset the Lions, too; their body language before the kick-off oozed concern. The Australia A in contrast bounced about like cocky, well, Australians.

It was about as bad a night as you could get. The Lions, particularly the forwards, performed as if they had been introduced five minutes before kick-off and they also lost Mike Catt, who had finally passed a fitness test the previous day. His continued presence on tour before Gosford – despite not taking part in a single training session – confirmed his importance to Henry's plans, but he pulled up with a recurrence of his calf injury while chasing a kick ahead and without an Australia A player in sight. Elsewhere, Dallaglio looked two yards off the pace, and the hooker Robin McBryde was also plainly unfit. His throwing-in, and that of his replacement Gordon Bulloch, was wayward to put it charitably and the Lions lost nine of their own line-outs – mainly to an uncapped Wallaby squad member called Justin Harrison, who was to become the Lions' *bete noire* in more ways than one.

Honiss also did his best to disrupt the Lions' continuity, penalising them constantly at the breakdown as if performing to an unseen prompt from Jones seated high in the stand. Phil Waugh, the Australia A captain and George Smith's main rival for the Wallabies' No 7 jersey, got away with murder.

The opening half was as ferocious as anything seen on tour, with Australia A piling into rucks as if their lives depended on it, but after finally getting into the Australia A territory the Lions promptly took the lead through a Neil Jenkins penalty. Jenkins kicked a second before half-time, but Jones as well as lobbing a few cynical missiles their way had also plainly done his homework on the Lions' midweek side. All he had to do was study a few videos of Wales in the Six Nations and see Jenkins standing flat to feed his crash ball centres. As the Wales captain Dai Young was also in charge of the tourists' second string and, allegedly, coaching them for much of the time while Henry and the others concentrated on the Test side, Jones had a perfect defensive blueprint. There was no doubt that the Welshman had figured prominently in the A team's offensive planning, too, Jones probably noticing that Jenkins is not the world's best tackler. The Australia A forwards ran at, and over, him in an uninterrupted stream, reminding Henry perhaps of one of his favourite motivational phrases: 'If you're not part of the steamroller you're part of the road'.

Three penalties for the A stand-off Manny Edmonds put the Lions behind for the first time on tour and they trailed 15–6 at half-time with the home side in almost total control.

Henry must have known it was not to be his night just after half-time when Austin Healey, on for Jenkins, chipped ahead for his chasing wing, who turned out to be the prop, Jason Leonard. The huge penalty count from the first half continued to climb and Edmonds took advantage. After a try from the A team wing Scott Staniforth Dallaglio was sin-binned with ten minutes to go, and typically – amazing how often this happens – this was the signal for an upturn in the Lions' work rate, and a revival. There were tries from Mark Taylor, Jason Robinson and Matt Perry, but Dawson could convert only two of them and also missed a penalty that would have tied the game. Even a draw would have been an injustice.

Of the Lions players, only Scott Quinnell looked a likely Test prospect and a similar thought had obviously occurred to Henry who immediately announced that from then on everything would be concentrated on the Test matches and the first-choice side, the midweek dirt-trackers being left to fend for themselves.

'Everyone is disappointed but it might bring us to reality very quickly about what this tour is all about. It could be a big positive in the long term,' he added hopefully. For Lions traditionalists, the abandonment of the midweek side was sacrilege, but under the circumstances – the burgeoning injury crisis, the lack of outright class available outside the first team and the shortage of time – he didn't seem to have much of a choice. Jones, who manages to look sneery even when he is smiling, said how pleased he was with the cleanliness of the game, but as was his wont then twisted the knife and added that 'due process' might spot a Ben Cohen tackle on Richard Graham, which left the full-back with a fractured cheekbone.

Fractured cheekbones were getting contagious and next day the Lions first-choice wing Dan Luger suffered an identical injury in a collision with team-mate Neil Back. The squad had been running through defensive drills when the two clashed heads and it was Luger who came off the worse. An operation welded the broken parts together, the only consolation for the player being that he was unable to fly for a week and had a few days in Manly's winter sunshine. Luger's was a total accident but those who had witnessed some of the brutal Lions contact sessions nodded: 'Told you so.'

The loss of the wing, another Test certainty, was a serious blow and a suddenly all eyes were turned on Jason Robinson; in a few months he had been elevated from England substitute to the man who could win a Test series. If this sudden promotion bothered the little Yorkshireman he didn't show it, hiding behind his wrap-round sunglasses and studiously keeping himself to himself.

A replacement centre was also needed for Catt with Scotland's Gregor Townsend considered a suitable candidate by the Scottish press and Scott Gibbs of Swansea and Wales by the Welsh. In the end the vote went to Gibbs and the Scots departed to sulk, a miserable 24 hours being completed when all three of the Scottish playing contingent were left out of the side to face NSW Waratahs on the following Saturday, this being immediately taken as an indication that they wouldn't make the Test side, either.

Henry explained: 'Scott and Gregor were the two names mentioned, and we decided to go for a specialist inside centre, because we only have one.' Townsend was thus free to continue his holiday in the Cayman Islands and may just have got the better side of the bargain. Catt, meanwhile, began to pack his bags with what looked suspiciously like relief. Before heading off for the airport he told us: 'I feel bad right now, but a calf injury is not the end of the world. I wouldn't have been able to live with myself if I hadn't tried to play, but the calf went the first time I really pushed it, and it is pretty demoralising.'

If Eddie Jones wasn't bad enough, the Lions next had to contend with Bob Dwyer, who had coached Leicester and Bristol in England before returning to Australia to take over New South Wales Waratahs and who, as we all knew by then, had been in charge of the Wallabies in 1989. He eventually guided them to World Cup victory two years later which just about earned him forgiveness for 1989, but the thought of anything in a red shirt obviously still rankled. I had met Dwyer at Murrayfield earlier that season when he arrived to publicise the game between his Barbarians side and Scotland. He seemed pleasant enough, but like the customs officer he did utter the old mantra of every Australian of a certain generation: 'Yes, you could say I remember 1989 well.' Back in Australia he also seemed to possess odd double standards, writing in the London *Sunday Times* about what a marvellous side the Lions were and then tearing them to pieces in his Australian newspaper columns.

The route to Sydney Football Stadium from Manly led through the famous red-light district of Paddington past pubs packed with red jerseys, dodgy night clubs and shop fronts bearing legends like 'Maddy the chemist of Paddy', but the atmosphere inside the ground was vile. Sydney Football Stadium had seen Campese's daft pass in 1989 and the famous cricket tied Test of 1960 or, as they like to say in Australia: That Pass and The Tied Test. Like Americans, Australians like their sporting moments defined and mythologised and Campese had even made That Pass into a sort of business venture, appearing in a spoof TV advert – like the England penalty chumps Stuart Pearce and Gareth Southgate – to demonstrate that he couldn't even pass a can of booze straight.

Sydney Football Stadium was also home for rugby league's Sydney Roosters, but on arrival it became clear that it was more like a bear pit. There was a brave attempt by the ARU to introduce some nostalgia into the proceedings with a parade of former Wallabies, with Campese himself, Michael Lynagh and Ken Catchpole making a lap of honour with varying degrees of sprightliness, but the mood of the crowd was inhospitable to say the least. Most of the British press filing that night were seated among Australian fans in a row of benches equipped with retractable wooden desk tops. There was an aisle leading to the nearest bar just behind and the occasion – some rugby match – was simply an excuse for a gargantuan drinking session. For half an hour before kick-off right up to the final whistle a constant stream of thirsty 'spectators' – male and female – staggered up and down the aisle ignoring the action on the field. An Australian across the passageway introduced himself and told me: 'It's great to have you in our country I hope you have a great stay', but his benevolence towards British visitors vanished the moment Martin Johnson came charging out of the tunnel, almost bowling over the venerable former Wallabies captain John Thornett on the way. As if throwing a switch my new friend immediately launched into a non-stop stream of invective aimed at the distant figures in red. 'Dirty Pommie bastards' and 'tear the bastard's arm off', that sort of thing. He paused at half-time to offer to buy me a drink and then continued in the same vein to the final whistle. In the seat on my right Barry Coughlan of the *Cork Examiner* maintained a similar continuous barrage of insults at fans passing on the way to the bar and when I stood up to pull out the mobile phone connection for my laptop modem the swing desk, like a medieval trebuchet, launched my computer into the row three tiers down. It was bedlam.

On the field, it was even worse. The referee, Scott Young, had obviously decided that this was a match that might require careful policing and had made his mind up to stamp his authority on proceedings from the start. In other words, the first act of foul play and the offender would be off. When the Waratahs kicked off, Grewcock rose to catch the ball and Tom Bowman, the New South Wales lock, came in with an elbow; Grewcock and Phil Vickery retaliated and when the kerfuffle died down Young raised the yellow card – in front of Bowman. This had taken all of thirty seconds and things, you could say, went downhill from there. In between the foul play it could be noticed that Jonny Wilkinson, Will Greenwood and Brian O'Driscoll were creating endless problems for the Waratahs defence, but the game will live longer in the memory of those unfortunate enough to witness it for an extraordinary, premeditated assault on the Irish stand-off Ronan O'Gara by the former Saracens player Duncan McRae, his sending-off, and four more yellow cards to go with that of Bowman. There was also the now-inevitable Lions injury, Greenwood hobbling off with ankle damage. He was never to play again on tour and as preparation for a meeting with Australia six days later Henry could hardly have done worse.

With Bowman off, Wilkinson moving to centre after the loss of Greenwood, and with four forwards later sin-binned, the match was a severely disjointed affair. And although the tourists produced some flowing rugby at times, the violence seemed to upset them far more than the home team. In the end, the Lions scored five tries and conceded four, most of these through a channel pointed at the makeshift centre, Wilkinson. On the positive side, Jason Robinson grabbed two more tries to bring his tour tally to eight and O'Driscoll was uncontainable at times. Dafydd James, the other Test wing candidate, defended well and also managed a try.

After the early departure of Bowman, the Lions scrum not surprisingly immediately demolished New South Wales in the first two set-pieces and after the second of these, O'Driscoll wriggled through the home midfield, Neil Back kept the ball alive for Robinson and O'Driscoll was on the end of the move for a run-in under the posts. Wilkinson converted and the Lions were 7–0 up in four minutes.

Waratahs flanker Stu Pinkerton ambled over untouched in the corner within a minute after some undisciplined Lions running in their own 22 and a dropped pass, but when Grewcock robbed New South Wales of possession at the other end, the lock's slick inside pass put Robinson in for his seventh try of the tour. 'Fucking little black bastard,' yelled the man across the aisle.

Another hint that this was no ordinary game of rugby

67

came when Vickery was penalised for punching the now-returned Bowman, and Manny Edmonds' kick was batted down by Grewcock under the posts. The Lions lost Greenwood, and much of their midfield invention, on 25 minutes, with O'Gara coming on at stand-off and Wilkinson moving sideways. As captain Martin Johnson was to point out with some understatement later: 'Jonny hasn't played there for a while and he defended a bit narrow at times.'

The Waratahs went offside for Wilkinson to kick his first penalty of the night and then, after scrum-half Matt Dawson glided past the opposition back row, Robinson picked up in the scrum-half position and jinked over past a mesmerised defence. But then came the home fightback, literally in the case of McRae. Wing Francis Cullimore got over in the corner after two blatant forward passes and then, at a breakdown on the Lions line, the arm of centre Sam Harris popped out of a pile of bodies for the Waratahs' third try. Edmonds converted to make the score 24–17 and put New South Wales within sight of a famous upset, but then came McRae's moment of madness.

Twenty minutes from time more animalistic yells from the aisle opposite signalled another incident and there was McRae, with the ball miles away, seated astride Ronan O'Gara, raining punches into his face. O'Gara retired bleeding profusely while McRae, having been shown the red card, strolled off with a huge grin on his face and to sympathetic applause. It didn't take a student of human nature to work out what was going to happen next and sure enough the next passage of play ended with skirmishes breaking out all over the field and the comical sight of Johnson caught in limbo and unsure which one to join in.

The touch judge recommended a mass sin-binning and Vickery and Grewcock of the Lions and Brendan Cannon and Cameron Blades of New South Wales were all shown the yellow card simultaneously. The match lost its structure totally with Young ordering uncontested scrums and simply adding to the disorder. But Wilkinson calmly kicked a penalty to restore some Lions equilibrium and then took a deft pass from Back to race over halfway out. At 27–17 it was virtually all over, and when Wood won a tight-head, James came off his wing to plunge over. Dawson kicked a superb conversion and Edmonds' late solo effort was an irrelevance, although the defeat was deemed to merit a New South Wales lap of honour presumably for their pugilistic skills.

All that remained then were the recriminations and accusations and while O'Gara was given eight stitches in the bowels of the stadium we convened gleefully for what looked like being a lively press conference, smacking our lips like customers at a cock fight. As well as the physical damage done deliberately to O'Gara and accidentally to Greenwood, there were the inevitable mental wounds which lingered long afterwards, helped by the pictures filling the following day's newspapers of the battered, bloody face of O'Gara. The outraged Lenihan drew more blood when he said: 'It was a disgrace. It was quite clear from the replays on television monitors that he (McRae) whacked Ronan four or five times on the ground. You could imagine the headlines in the papers here tomorrow if one of our players had behaved like McRae.' The manager also expressed surprise that O'Gara had also been called before a citing commission.

Henry added: 'There were a number of unsavoury incidents, and under the circumstances I am proud of the discipline that the players showed. I think they showed commendable restraint.'

Dwyer and his captain Phil Waugh were next up and Dwyer produced an extraordinary performance. He would not condemn McRae, insisting that he was simply retaliating to an assault by O'Gara, the smallest and lightest and least belligerent of the Lions party by a long way. Dwyer then claimed McRae may have learned a penchant for over-reaction in England where he had played for Saracens and then added that O'Gara 'gave up' after the first blow, implying the Lions were really pussy cats after all. He then produced his gem. Asked if the violence had been premeditated, he said: 'If I were to pick someone to rough the Lions up it would not have been Duncan McRae.' The temptation was to ask Dwyer who he would have chosen, but the arrival of some Lions to give their version of events brought his little cameo to a close.

The Lions hardly did themselves any favours, either, and one of the nastiest moments in a night of some repugnance belonged to Austin Healey, who had played for exactly sixty seconds as replacement for Jonny Wilkinson, but obviously felt it his duty to appear at the press conference. As Dwyer tried without much success to defend himself, McRae and his team, Healey could be seen gesticulating at NSW team officials, among whom was Strath Gordon, the senior ARU media and communications manager. The Englishman was making pointed gestures at his own backside to indicate what he thought of Dwyer's comments. The tourists thus lost much of the moral high ground and the evening ended in high farce when Dwyer realised he had left his bag at the table and had to return to retrieve it just as Grewcock was in full flow describing the New South Wales brutality.

Healey was later to make matters even worse when he wrote of McRae in *The Observer*: 'The boys really hope they get the chance to play against him in England,' forgetting perhaps that the last time McRae played in England he had suffered broken ribs after an incident in a club game against Leicester, an incident that ended in a lengthy ban for Martin Johnson.

Healey might as well have taken a full-page advertisement in *The Australian* to announce 'I AM TROUBLE' and if those coming across him for the first time thought that here was a dangerously loose cannon, careening uncontrollably from one side of the ship to the other, they were to be proved absolutely right.

KNOW YOUR ENEMY

D espite the evidence of the video footage and the fact that Duncan McRae had been cited and banned for seven weeks the New South Wales match seemed to confirm what the Australian press had wanted to believe all along: the Lions were going to replay 1989 all over again and the Test series would disintegrate into a bloody war of attrition. The tourists were to employ 'biff' to quell Wallaby flair, just as they had done at the Battle of Ballymore twelve years earlier. Events at the Brisbane Test were, to put it in the local vernacular, 'going to kick off big style'; the Gabba would erupt into 'a slugfest'. Channel 7's sports programme on the Sunday morning – usually given over almost exclusively to rugby league and Australian Rules football, although they claimed to be 2001 Wallabies sponsors – took voyeuristic delight in showing the television footage of McRae seated astride O'Gara and pummelling the Irishman's face. As the replay faded, with a grinning McRae walking slowly off the field, the presenter remarked: 'Well, those Lions sure came out fighting.' One of the studio guests, a former Aussie Rules footballer, asked in the strident, gormless manner endemic in programmes like these: 'I can't see what all the fuss is about. What's a little claret between friends?' The Australian Sunday newspapers, while condemning McRae's assault, also highlighted Dwyer's claim that Danny Grewcock sparked the mayhem by throwing a punch at Tom Bowman in the first minute. Bowman had simply retaliated. Dwyer, whose professorial looks disguise the instincts of an alley cat, also weighed in with a spirited attack on Henry in his newspaper column in the *Sunday Times*, as usual drawing on his long Australian memory and invoking the lessons of history: 'You can take the boy out of New Zealand, but you can't take New Zealand out of

71

the boy,' wrote Dwyer. 'I am reminded of the infamous incident in which Henry's fellow New Zealander, the former All Blacks coach Laurie Mains, vehemently defended his arch-villain prop, Richard Loe, after he dropped an elbow into Paul Carozza's face in a Test against Australia in 1992. It seems New Zealanders find it difficult to see any wrong from their own sides.' In other words, it was all Henry's fault for being born a Kiwi. There was also some scoffing about Lenihan's 'whingeing' in the British press about the orchestrated home media campaign against the Lions. Eddie Jones, the nation's rugby rent-a-quote, weighed in in his inimitable way, accusing the Lions of 'treading on guys, going in after the tackle and hitting players'. Even when guilty the Australians managed to adopt the role of innocents; they were winning the propaganda war hands down.

And like a Kremlin interrogation – hard soft, soft hard – the tour went on. Australia A and New South Wales were to be followed by a midweek match on Tuesday June 26 against New South Wales Country Cockatoos at the International Stadium in Coffs Harbour, a holiday resort on the east coast midway between Brisbane and Sydney. This involved another short internal flight with the press booked on to the same private charter as the players, to the undisguised displeasure of the management. With McBryde heavily strapped, Dallaglio moving painfully slowly and with what looked suspiciously like a limp from Keith Wood in the departure lounge of Sydney International Airport, the Lions were beginning to resemble Napoleon's Old Guard after the Battle of Waterloo. The one exception was a remarkably relaxed Martin Johnson, who with his faithful deputy Wood in tow, shambled over to our coffee table to demand of the Scottish contingent: 'Name a Scottish football team with J in it.' It was then we recalled the Lions' official media guide and the revelation that Johnson was a trivia buff. The shock of seeing a human side to this fearful man was almost physical. Wood also caused a stir among the Scots by revealing that his fiancee was from Scotland and that any future little Woodses would qualify for Scotland.

The first sight of the opposition en masse came at the press accommodation in the All Seasons Premier Pacific Bay Resort, which was also the chosen home base and training camp for the Wallabies. Macqueen had long encouraged a family atmosphere among his players and wives, children and girlfriends were positively encouraged, giving the lie to the old sporting theory that a celibate fighter is a hungry, winning fighter. Not surprisingly, the Lions – who were out training within half an hour of landing – were quartered in the Coffs Harbour Novotel three kilometres away. They couldn't afford repeats of some of the embarrassment that occurred on the first visit to Brisbane, when some of the Queensland players had also been lodged in the Sheraton. This led to some unnecessarily awkward – but quite hilarious – situations and at one point the Lions loose-head prop Tom Smith and his Queensland opposite number Glenn Panoho were spotted stalking each other round the vast hotel foyer in an effort to avoid being trapped in the same lift together.

The All Seasons was another stunning four-star resort with forty acres of land surrounding a group of apartments and its attractions included a restaurant and bar overlooking a man-made lake, Charlie Bananas Kids Club, billiard room, squash and tennis courts, three heated pools, a nine-hole golf course and a health and fitness centre containing instructions and warning signs from the Coffs Harbour disciples of the Australian nanny state: 'Do not put weights on bench', 'don't drop weights on the floor' and, alarmingly, 'patrons must bring a towel to use equipment'. There were more cautionary signs than apparatus.

The resort's other main marketing point could be seen at one end of the hotel lobby close to a large sign that proclaimed: 'Coffs Harbour, Home to the Vodafone Wallabies' and where a huge, glass-encased courtyard closeted a number of large men in green and gold tracksuits. The curious among us could watch them eating and drinking and playing with their children and occasionally talking to wives or partners in full public view but with the obvious unstated proviso that you could look but not touch, or even talk to them. As they moved about their daily business among the indoor plants and trees with that deliberate slow-motion lassitude of professional athletes everywhere I was reminded irresistibly – and this is intended to be more descriptive of their habitat than their appearance or character – of school trips to Manchester's Belle Vue Zoo and the magnificent reptile house there.

Later that evening those of us employed by Sunday newspapers were given cause to give thanks for large mercies: Alex Broun arrived hot foot from the Novotel to announce that Lawrence Dallaglio was out of the tour and that Ireland's David Wallace would join the party as a replacement. Broun, as was his habit, paused to let this sink in before producing another bombshell or two: Keith Wood was struggling with a knee injury and Will Greenwood's ankle ligament damage had ruled him out of contention for a place in the weekend's First Test. Wood's disability was a serious worry, but the other news was hardly a surprise, simply the confirmation of what many had feared. By this time it was around 11p.m. and the daily newspapers and the radio journalists, having wined and dined in their usual lavish fashion, had to file stories. Those of us not governed by daily deadlines returned to the bar, our only regrets being that we couldn't tune in to some of the radio reports. It can't be easy to pronounce cruciate-ligament damage after a bottle or two of Jacob's Creek Sauvignon Blanc.

On the positive side, Wallace did make history by becoming the third member of his family (brothers Richard and Paul were tourists in 1993 and 1997 respectively) to become a British Lion while the England hooker Dorian West, at the advanced old age of 33, was called up as cover for Robin McBryde, Gordon Bulloch and Wood. West thus became the fifth hooker employed on tour, another world record.

Both Wallace and West, understandably, had not been

seated by their telephones at home waiting for the call from Lenihan. Wallace had been in Copenhagen en route to Poland for an Ireland training camp while West had been alerted by Martin Johnson just after he had landed in Minorca for a holiday with his wife and two daughters. He had dropped them off at their rented villa before heading back to Mahon airport, clad in just shorts and sandals. Mrs West, apparently, did not see the funny side, but the swift arrival of both replacements in Coffs Harbour within twenty-four hours is surely a tribute to modern air travel and the worth of mobile phones. Other welcome late arrivals at Coffs Harbour were the former Lions captains Willie John McBride and Finlay Calder, both of whom were employed by different tour package companies. The temptation was to ask if they had brought their boots. The arrival of Calder was potentially the most useful *aide memoire* yet to those few Australians who might be beginning to forget 1989 and explained why he was determined to keep a low profile. The Lions management, it must also be said, were not exactly overjoyed to see him.

On the Monday before the match against the NSW Country XV the Wallabies came out of their glass enclosure to meet the press. The venue was a huge marquee close to the resort's lake and alongside the tennis courts and a dozen players filed in with Macqueen and the management to face the microphones, cameras and notebooks. After dominating the Super 12 series, the ACT Brumbies provided the bulk of the 31-man Wallaby squad and the top table groaned with the likes of the ubiquitous George Smith, the great Stephen Larkham, the monolithic Owen Finegan and the tiny Andrew Walker, the former rugby league player who would be facing the equally terrier-like Jason Robinson on the wing. Centre Rod Kafer, who had gone into print a fortnight earlier to castigate the Australian selectors for showing a bias towards Queenslanders, was missing and it transpired that he had been discarded all together. This was a sharp riposte to a disaffected player and one that the Lions would have done well to have emulated later. In Kafer's place, the Australians had brought in Nathan Grey, straight off their production line of tough-tackling, robust, 100kg Wallaby backs.

Macqueen was plainly the man in charge. Unlike the Lions hierarchy at press conferences where Lenihan sat in the middle dominating proceedings and Henry placed himself shyly at the end of the table, the Australian coach was in the centre with his disciples spread out on either side. John McKay, the Wallabies' Lenihan counterpart, sat at the end. Macqueen certainly had a presence, possibly something to do with the fact that in real life he was a successful, millionaire-status, businessman. Rugby needed him more than he needed rugby. This also made him a bit of an oddity in his own country and could have caused problems because Australians on the whole don't like 'tall poppies'. But a glance at his biography confirmed that Macqueen fitted the favourite Aussie stereotype of a battler made good. He had been a lifeguard and surfboat rower and had also recovered from a brain tumour eleven years previously. As well as being an indisputable good egg, he was also unarguably the best rugby coach around and obviously a shrewd operator.

It was Macqueen who had originally introduced the ritual of a former Wallaby presenting the captain with his jersey and speaking to the team before each Test and he also once took the team to a dawn service on a First World War French battlefield on Remembrance Day in 1998. It was said he flew an Australian flag in his garden. He obviously understood the Australian psyche.

His coaching career had begun with junior representative teams before taking over the Warringah first grade side from where he stepped into senior ranks with Sydney, New South Wales B and the NSW Waratahs. He became an Australian selector, coached an Australian XV to a 57–8 win over Ireland and then became the first coach of the new

Super 12 side, the ACT Brumbies, in 1996. From there he had never looked back, winning the 1999 World Cup with the Wallabies and virtually everything else since. The Lions would round the set off very nicely.

At Coffs Harbour Macqueen took the floor first and proceeded to go straight into a routine which I recognised at once as what some English pundits have labelled rather cruelly as the Sweaty Socks (Jocks) Syndrome. This is a deliberate attempt to put your team into the role of underdog, the little guys battling impossible odds. Scotland down the years had made this into an art form almost, producing the most outrageous performances against impossible odds, particularly against the English. Faced with opposition like Italy and the unaccustomed role of favourites, Scotland almost invariably blew it. In Australia they know this as 'the rat up the drainpipe theory'. In other words, Australia would only pull their fingers out only when the odds were against them, when 'the rat started running up the drainpipe'. Macqueen immediately set about the task of trying to convince us that despite winning every trophy possible in the previous twelve months and facing a scratch team picked from four different nations on home soil and a squad already stricken by injuries, Australia were somehow rank outsiders.

We were no strangers to this by now. Andrew Slack, the Wallabies selector and former captain, had kicked it all off earlier when he said: 'Hand on heart, I think the Lions will start favourites.' Macqueen followed suit, insisting that 'we are about to encounter Australian rugby's greatest challenge' and that 'the Lions will be the best-prepared opposition Australia has ever faced'.

He did, however, end with an implicit warning: 'We pick a goal for ourselves every year,' he said. 'Two years ago it was the World Cup, last year it was the Tri Nations. This year it's the Lions and this is the most motivated I have seen this Wallaby team.' There was no attempt by Macqueen, either, to continue the slagging that had

77

characterised the previous week, the Aussie coach simply expressing the wish that it was 'a good, hard, clean game'. But then again, Jones, Dwyer and a dozen others had done all that sort of stuff for him. It was no surprise to discover later that Jones, as well as coaching the Brumbies and Australia A, had been heavily involved in the Wallabies' preparation, with his main responsibility obviously for outrageous spin-doctoring.

After the formal press conference we were free to talk to any individual Wallaby player, who stood around on their own at convenient distances inside and outside the marquee. They had plainly done all this before and most of the interviews went swimmingly. The Walker and Robinson clash was an obvious 'angle' and the Australian wing found himself besieged with the same question, about league returnees thrown head to head, to which he gave virtually the same answer: 'Mate, I have never played against Jason, but he is a great player and I am very much looking forward to lining up against him. Rugby league is so high here and Jason is a hero. Everyone knows about him and, whoever he plays for, he gives 100 per cent. He's quick, he has all the skills and he's a strong bloke. It would be a great test if I have to mark him, but it would be a highlight for me to play against a world-class player like him. If I do, I'll treasure the moment. If I am selected.' If I am selected; they all said that.

Larkham, like opposite number Jonny Wilkinson, looked like a schoolboy who had strayed in to look for autographs and he told an extraordinary story about a recent eye operation to correct myopia; apparently he was blind as a bat and most of his past great deeds – try-making breaks and last-minute drop goals – had been made with blurred vision. I remembered that Scott Gibbs and Brian O'Driscoll both wore spectacles and didn't use contact lenses for matches. Were their moments of rugby genius really a case of having no idea where they were going?

All the Wallabies seemed reassuringly ordinary, boring

almost, the only one with anything approaching an individual idiosyncrasy being Daniel Herbert, the Jack Palance lookalike capped forty-eight times in the centre for his country. Herbert had a disconcerting, oddly menacing, habit of looking at interviewers with his head turned forty-five degrees to the side, but with eyes fixed unblinkingly on you, as if he were sighting a weapon. Someone later said he was deaf in one ear.

The nearest thing the Wallabies had to an old-fashioned enforcer, à la Steve Finnane, was Owen Finegan, also known mysteriously as 'Melon'. Finegan had been suspended and missed the Brumbies' Super 12 final win after stomping on his Wallaby team-mate Michael Foley in the semi-final against Queensland, so was obviously not a man to ask about the origin of his nickname, but he was happy to discuss his roots for the sake of one of the Irish journalists. As he talked about his family from the old country his eyes grew misty and his Australian accent turned perilously close to bog Irish. Only an unromantic question about the Lions back row stopped him from bursting into a chorus of 'I'll take you home again, Kathleen'.

I did my bit, again remembering the first law of interviewing, that of finding some common ground. I had gathered some background research from the Wallabies handbook which contained brief biographies along with a picture of all the players and coaching staff. But the presence of so much greatness can scramble the mind. I approached Rod Moore, the New South Wales prop and asked him how he fancied his chances against the magnificent Tom Smith. 'Actually, mate, I'm Ewen McKenzie the assistant coach,' said Moore. I spotted the highly recognisable figure of Mark Ella and hastened across to tell him I had seen him play on the all-conquering 1984 Wallabies tour of Britain. 'Actually, mate, I'm Glenn, Mark's brother, assistant coach with responsibility for the backs. But don't worry lots of people make that mistake.' Joe Roff, the winger who had signed a contract with Biarritz for the next season, giggled nervously

– as you do in the presence of the unbalanced – when I mentioned that I had been to Biarritz and that in terms of its sea, sand and surfing it was really Manly with croissants. Roff had the grace to admit that he was moving to France for the money and had, so far, learned no French.

The common denominator of the Wallabies – at least the ones they presented to us – was that they were totally relaxed, co-operative and charming. They looked and acted like winners, which of course they were. All of them, in character, outlook and temperament, in fact, were slightly inferior clones of their towering captain, the 79-times capped John Eales, who was in his tenth year as an Australian internationalist. Down that decade the mighty Eales had won numerous man-of-the-match awards, scored winning tries, kicked winning goals, received a host of honours including the Order of Australia and displayed a humility and sheer niceness that was hard to credit at times. The Australians liked to portray him as the quintessential Australian sportsman, which of course he was not, being free of braggadocio and well mannered in victory and defeat. Wally Lewis, Ian Chappell or David Campese, he definitely was not.

Everyone has a favourite story about the Eales generosity of spirit, and I will mention this one: the Wallabies had come to Murrayfield for an autumn international in 2000 where Eales made a point of meeting Struan Kerr Liddell, a young forward from the Lismore club in Edinburgh, who had been rendered a tetraplegic in a scrummaging accident. That should have been that; any player can perform acts of charity when cameras are present but, a day before the final Test in Sydney, John Evans, the organiser of the Struan Appeal, was astonished to receive an e-mail from Eales to say that he was sending a Wallaby jersey, signed by all the team, over for auction. The fact that he would think of this twenty-four hours before a deciding Test match was mind-boggling. Asked how he would like to be remembered, Eales had once said: 'As a bloke who fulfilled his potential in the game, had a great deal of fun, and gave it everything he had in him.' He was almost too good to be true and apparently his team-mates had christened him 'Nobody', as in 'Nobody's Perfect'. It seemed far too subtle a nickname for an Aussie sportsman and Eales always claimed the story was apocryphal, but it certainly fitted. The Australian captain who, with his narrowed eyes and noble features, resembles a hero from a Western film, was vying with Martin Johnson for the unofficial title of finest lock in the world and, although there seemed little to choose between them in terms of leadership qualities or performing the day-to-day business of being a rugby forward, the general feeling was that you'd always pick Johnson as your partner in a street fight and be happy to take Eales home to meet your mother.

The Australian performance had been in stark contrast to the Lions' media efforts and as they drifted back slowly to the Wallaby House I wondered, not for the first time: who exactly are the good guys here? Basking in the shared bonhomie and gazing around the sublime surroundings, I turned to an Australian journalist and remarked: 'They seem really nice blokes.' He looked at me as with that mix of pity and scorn that only an Australian can produce. 'Mate, you must be joking. They're a bunch of spin-doctoring bastards. They'll be as nice as pie to you because the ARU want to show you what perfect hosts they will make for the 2003 World Cup. You think you have it bad with the Lions, but we can't get close to the Wallabies. They have training sessions behind padlocked gates, security guards and you can't get into the dressing rooms. You can't talk to players before and after games. Believe me, they'll drop you like a hot potato once the series is over.'

Suddenly it struck home: the sun, the water, the free drinks, the charm, this had all the insidious qualities of an elaborate seduction. All that was missing was Ravel's *Bolero* in the background. I could feel hoary Australian hands creeping slowly up my thigh. Three weeks later, when the job was done, Macqueen and Eales kept the British press waiting two hours at Stadium Australia and we had been spurned like unwanted lovers.

That evening most of us were all back in the same marquee, this time to meet James Robson, the Lions doctor, for an impromptu press conference. The optimistic among us hoped he might spill some beans about the burgeoning injury toll and put it down to the consequence of the training. 'Lions Doctor Slams Management Style', we could almost write the dream headline there and then. The contrast from earlier in the day could not have been more marked. The sun had gone down and it was chilly inside the tent. Most of the table and chairs had gone, as had the free drinks. Half an hour went by as we sat there waiting for the arrival of Dr Robson, forty-five minutes. Was he just like Lenihan and the rest? Finally, as we shivered in the gloaming the mobile phone of Peter Jackson, the *Daily Mail* rugby writer – the usual conduit between Broun and the rest of us – rang. Jackson listened for a few moments, then told us the news: there had been an accident. Anton Toia, one of the Lions baggage handlers, was dead and Robson would not be arriving to meet the media. Toia, the genial, jovial, chain-smoking Maori father of two had become an integral part of daily life Down Under for players and management and was one of the few members of the backroom staff willing to give the media the time of day. Apparently he died of a heart attack in the Opal Cove surf close to the team hotel after he jumped out of the boat to swim to shore while returning from a whale-watching expedition. Robson had tried to resuscitate him, but failed. Broun later arrived in reception for an informal briefing and infuriatingly mentioned that three of the Lions players – he did not give their names – were being questioned by the local police. He certainly knew how to tantalise the scribes.

I wondered how the Lions players would react to the death of Anton. He had worked with Scotland and Ireland in the past and all the 'Celts' got on famously with him.

Scott Gibbs knew him from as far back as the Welsh tour of Australia in 1991. Would this tour, which long before had lost the concept of a simple series of sporting contests, and now seemed inspired by the same sort of zealotry that guided medieval crusades, have some sanity restored by a death in the family? Would players and management begin to realise that maybe winning wasn't everything? Some words from Steve Black were reassuring: 'I couldn't ever imagine not being in an environment where winning didn't mean everything, but it was when I was lifting Anton's body on to the stretcher that it struck home again that there are more important things. Anton was a lovely, lovely man, and the lads had a lot of affection for him. It was when I saw him lying there that I thought: "Hang on a minute. Maybe life's not just about victory on the rugby field. Maybe we need to get some sort of balance here."' Even Black, however, the most human of the management staff, concluded the chat with the words: 'Everything's all about winning in the end, isn't it?'

The status of the NSW Country Cockatoos, the Lions' next opposition, was perhaps best summed up by the driver, from Coffs Harbour, who was to ferry the press to the ground. As we climbed aboard he asked: 'Who's playing today?' The International Stadium turned out to be a bit of a non sequitur as the Lions match was the first international to be staged there and after Gosford and Sydney Football Stadium it was something of a culture shock.

Inside what was normally a cricket ground, the crowd on the far side were about four hundred metres from the action, the touchline itself being defined by a straggling row of sponsors' hoardings. Not surprisingly, as radio telescopes had not been provided, some of the fans over there got a bit restless. The press facilities were non-existent and the journalists' work area was a marquee the size of one of a Blacks frame tent in the car park. Some light relief did come in the shape of an advert for a local brothel in the official match programme which promised a 'variety of ladies for your pleasure' and 'most major credit cards accepted'. The country XV, and their substitutes, arrived in a 15-seater mini-bus. This was rugby at its coarsest, and extremely welcome for that.

Drawn from the whole of New South Wales, they were all amateurs and some had travelled over one hundred miles to get there. Bernie Klasen, their captain, bred chickens and this was the highlight of his long career. 'We sang the national anthem in the changing room and there were a few blokes in tears,' he said. 'There's great pride in Country rugby.' As with any other Australian team facing a foreign foe, there was plenty of support. Ewen McKenzie, the Australian assistant coach, and the New South Wales and Wallaby prop Cameron Blades offered their help in preparing the Country pack while Eales presented them with their jerseys. Again there was that feeling that all Australians were prepared to pull together in a common cause.

Despite the 3p.m. start and the welcome sunshine there was a pall detectable in the air and although the Lions duly beat the Country XV 46–3 it was a performance almost as doom-laden as Broun's news of the previous evening. The game may have been a dire affair with the Lions unable to impose themselves on a surprisingly efficient bunch of amateurs, but there were more welcome lighter moments. Bob Dwyer was seated in the stand behind us with his family and looked in remarkably good spirits, or maybe he was simply laughing at the incompetence of the Lions. As with every other stadium in Australia trespassing on to the pitch was looked upon in the same light as bag-snatching or rape and dire warnings about the consequences were issued sternly by the PA announcer throughout the game. At humble Coffs Harbour the penalty was $500 and a severe ticking-off, whereas at Stadium Australia offenders who invaded the golden turf faced a $5,000 penalty, a public flogging and deportation on the next available flight. A morbid fear of having their grass trampled on seemed to grip Australia and, when the Lions played Queensland at Ballymore, interlopers were treated with quite alarming violence by stewards.

At Coffs Harbour, however, all the strictures could not stop one brave and naked Lions fan from the far end of the ground – possibly because he could see nothing of the match – streak across to the TV gantry and climb this ahead of the baffled security. Another couple of fans in fancy dress were marched off by the grim-faced Coffs Harbour constabulary to some unspecified fate.

On the field, meanwhile, Scott Gibbs made his debut, along with the other late arrivals David Wallace and Tyrone Howe. Dorian West was on the bench. As might be expected, their performances were mixed. Gibbs and Martin Corry – again – looked as if they were, in the words of Henry 'holding their hands up for a Test place', but the others were way off the pace. There was one impressive, blistering run of maybe thirty metres right in front of the main grandstand by the replacement wing Howe, but unfortunately he was two yards outside the touchline. Some of the Irish journalists who had believed the logical wing substitute was Leinster's Denis Hickie, raised their eyebrows and nodded their heads at each other with gestures that said: 'Didn't I tell you as much?' The first of the six Lions tries did not come until nearly thirty minutes had passed, Gibbs, Corry and Martyn Williams creating the space for Ben Cohen to finish from forty metres. Another three followed from Charvis, Gibbs and Austin Healey, who dummied over from a close-range ruck. As the game disintegrated in a shower of replacements, Dai Young forced his way over after strong play by Malcolm O'Kelly and a long pass set Cohen free for his second try and the fiftieth Lions touchdown in six matches. But though the Lions pressed hard for the rest of the match, their work was tepid and the Country boys put up a spirited defensive performance. The referee Greg Hinton, another Australian official keen to impose his feeble presence on the match, hardly helped matters with over forty penalties. On the whole the Lions' performance was startlingly inept and even Dwyer left long before the end.

To the huge delight of the Australian press crammed into the marquee after the match, Henry was goaded into a long moan about the universal home tactic of the miss-pass that goes behind advancing players, a move that he deemed as outright obstruction. This was a well-known tactic in rugby league and every other side the Lions had met in Australia had done exactly the same thing, so it was hardly a surprise and the feeling was the Lions should have been prepared for anything. The Cockatoos coach, for his part, insisted that the difference between his team and the professionals was the time devoted to training and individual preparation, rather than skill levels. He may well have had a point.

On the last day in Coffs Harbour it began to rain, the downpour failing to deter Robinson from a full-contact session lasting two and a half hours. The rain did, however, produce some encouraging noises in the Lions camp. If it was raining in Coffs Harbour it could be raining in Brisbane, and the British were used to playing in rain, the Wallabies were not. This is another rugby fallacy with a similar basis in fact as the famous fly-half factory somewhere in Wales, that only Scots and New Zealanders know how to ruck, the All Black haka is not intended to be intimidatory and that every England player went to public school. But to most it appeared the Lions could do with all the help they could get. Australia hadn't played together since June 9, when they beat New Zealand Maori, but some felt the rest would do them no harm. It was also true that Brisbane's Gabba was as alien to the Wallabies as it was to the Lions. A rugby union Test had never been played there and even Macqueen was moved to admit: 'One of the dilemmas we have is that, wherever we train or play, we don't get a great home-grown advantage.' But really these seemed to be fragile arguments in favour of the tourists. There were also injuries and loss of form among the Lions, factors that had not affected the Australians . . . yet.

The evening after the Cockatoos match Henry sat down with the management selection panel – Johnson, Robinson, Larder and Lenihan were the others – to choose the 22-man squad for the Test match. There was a large query over the full-back position, where Iain Balshaw had had another shocker that afternoon and Matt Perry still seemed the safe choice. The Cockatoos were supposed to be the medium for the recovery of Balshaw's confidence, but the move had backfired.

In 1997, the Lions players had learned about their selection or otherwise for the Tests via a letter pushed under their doors in the early hours of the morning. Black, for one, considered this, in his own words 'a cop-out' and it was decided that all the players would be gathered in one of the Coffs Harbour Novotel suites where Lenihan would read the names out. This, naturally caused a measure of suspense, particularly in the front row who would be named last. Lenihan started at 15 and worked downwards to one so it took only two names to end the outside chance Balshaw had of playing either at full-back or in the No 14, right wing jersey which was his other favoured position. The tour was turning rapidly into a nightmare for a youngster who had started the tour as one of the Lions' main attacking options. Henry admitted the player was suffering from a crisis of confidence but could not enlighten us on what he and the other coaches intended to do about it. 'He would be the first to admit he is not playing as well as he would like', Henry added with classic understatement.

The selection contained few surprises. Neil Back had bruised ribs and was not considered and his Leicester team-mate Martin Corry made the quantum leap from unwanted and unselected to playing the world champions within a month. The Leicester player was named on the blindside of the scrum leaving Richard Hill to move over to the open-side and take on the well-defined menace of

George Smith. Balshaw's Bath team-mate Perry, the man he displaced from the England side the previous season, was selected in his place and Tom Smith, to the undisguised relief of the Scottish press corps, was named as loose-head prop, a reward for his remarkable mobility and past Lions deeds. With Greenwood and Catt out, Rob Henderson was teamed with Brian O'Driscoll in the centre and nine months after taking up rugby union, and still to be named in an England starting XV, there was a first Lions cap for Jason Robinson, with Welshman Dafydd James taking the other wing slot.

In all, the team was made up of eight Englishmen – five in the pack – three Welsh, three Irish and one Scot and Henry had few doubts about their ability: 'I think that this team will produce a marvellous performance on Saturday. The attitude and commitment is total, and I am sure the players will produce a performance they can be proud of.'

There was little doubt who Henry saw as his trump card, the man who hadn't even made the initial selection of sixty-seven: 'Jason Robinson has been superb. He is a creator, someone who looks for work and pops up in unusual positions. He keeps defences guessing, he is a workhorse and not someone who is straddled by the history or tradition of rugby union. He has been a revelation on tour.'

Australia named their team on the same day with full-back Matt Burke dropped from the starting team for the first time in five years. Andrew Walker would take over the goalkicking role. 'We know that is perhaps our greatest challenge, and we have trained accordingly with that in mind,' said Macqueen in a final, desperate effort to establish Australia as the underdogs. 'The Lions have had a very good preparation, with six games under their belt since they've been out here. We've had one (against New Zealand Maori), and that is a very telling statistic.'

After the official press conferences the scribes departed to their rooms to put up a sign reading: 'Do Not Disturb. Parochialism At Work'. One Welsh paper unearthed the news that Corry really qualified for Wales through a Llandudno-born mum and she had wanted him to play for them. This was some measure of consolation for the omission from the starting XV of Neil Jenkins, Gibbs, Charvis and virtually everybody else. The Irish had a field day with a bewildering number of news opportunities, but dwelling almost exclusively on the partnership of Henderson and O'Driscoll while the West Country newspapers made great play about the Cornishman playing for Gloucester, Phil Vickery. The insular nature of newspaper reporting was perhaps best summed up by the *Wigan Observer* which broke the habit of a lifetime to give some space to rugby union and the fact that 'former Wigan star' Jason Robinson was on the wing for the British Lions. The Scots turned gratefully to their old saviour Smith, the man who had rescued us from the ignominy of not having a single player in a Lions' starting XV.

On the Wednesday after the Cockatoos match and seven hours after the Test team announcement we were cramming into the tiny airport at Coffs Harbour for the last flight to Brisbane. There was a surprise waiting there – Macqueen and maybe a dozen of his players waiting for the same flight and looking, as ever, remarkably relaxed. Glenn Panoho, the eighteen-stones prop, cradled his young baby as if it was a piece of Waterford crystal and John Muggleton, the defensive coach, recognised us and said a cheery hello. He had heard the Lions line-up and thought it 'a pretty good team. You will obviously start as favourites.' And there was Daniel Herbert looking his team-mate Matt Cockbain in the eye, but with his head pointed at Gate 15.

They were all remarkably quiet on the flight, like particularly well-behaved schoolboys, and with none of the high jinks and banter normally associated with rugby players. Whether this was ingrained, or simply the presence of Macqueen, remained unclear. Larkham was seated behind me with his girlfriend and didn't speak a word to her the whole flight, but if this was tension it was soon dispelled by a remarkable cabaret act from Stephanie, the Ansett air hostess. Remarkably vivacious and loquacious she made a pleasant change from the resolutely butch male flight attendants employed by Qantas we had become accustomed to. She chattered away to a smiling Macqueen non-stop and at Brisbane, after a less than perfect touchdown, she remarked gleefully to the passengers: 'What a bloody awful landing.' British Airways was never like this. When she wished us goodbye over the intercom she added: 'I was going to wish the Wallabies good luck but then I thought it might look a bit too biased.' Stephanie's performance brought back smiling memories of Finlay Calder's tale of a Scottish tour of Australia and a similar internal flight. The players were getting on famously with the stunning air hostess, so much so that some were even considering asking for her telephone number. It was then she piped up: 'Are you guys rugby players? My husband played rugby.'

Yes, right, and who did he play for?

'Well, he did play for Australia.'

And what's his name?

'Steve Finnane.'

The Lions were back in the Sheraton, Brisbane, and the official press conference on the Friday before the Test was mobbed, with maybe 150 journalists shoe-horned into the hotel suite. It started in the usual fashion with Lenihan's injury update; this time McBryde was going home. There was some desultory quizzing about the selection and the gathering was enlivened by Henry's best one-liner of the tour. One of the Aussie journalists asked him: 'What do you say about grumpy Lions?' and the New Zealander replied: 'A load of rubbish, is that grumpy enough for you?'

Lenihan mentioned that the management might recruit a former Lion for some unspecified pre-match cheerleading. Who on earth could he mean? There were indeed a small army of former Lions in Brisbane that night, but few with

90

that sort of status. Calder certainly qualified as a winning captain in Australia but in the light of the bad press about 1989 it may not have been considered politically expedient to ask him. The Australians would have made a real meal of that and the discovery that Calder was to address the Lions pre-match would simply have confirmed their worst fears. In the end, it turned out to be four-times Lions tourist Willie John McBride. Calder contented himself with pushing a note of encouragement under Johnson's bedroom door. Down in the lobby meanwhile, Jason Robinson was given a personal pep talk by a corpulent British fan who turned out, on closer examination, to be the former England captain Will Carling.

Other opposition was in town that weekend and more reminders that the Lions tour was of somewhat peripheral interest in Brisbane. The 'footie' game between Brisbane Lions and Hawthorn, and the deciding match in the State of Origin rugby league best-of-three between Queensland and New South Wales, relegated the test to a dismal third place in the local media pecking order. Or maybe fifth, if you counted the progress of Lleyton Hewitt and Pat Rafter at Wimbledon and the build-up to cricket's Ashes series. When the Lions and Wallabies arrived at the Gabba on the Friday, they found the cricket ground marked for the Australian Rules game that night with no sign of any goalposts or even the location of the benches. They did manage a short training session, but even Macqueen reported that the Wallabies had been denied access to the Brisbane Lions' personal dressing rooms, presumably because they wanted to keep them pristine for the fastidious Aussie Rules footballers that evening. This seemed astonishing insularity from the governors of the daftest team sport in the world, a game constructed from all the worst elements of rugby, gaelic football and soccer, and one that only Australians play. A measure of the skill level of 'footie' is best illustrated by recalling that all those macho, sun-tanned Aussies in their cut-away vests regularly take a hammering from a bunch of knock-kneed, pale-skinned, ginger-headed Gaelic footballers in their annual cross-code challenge match. There was more proof that the Lions had failed to make much of a local impact in the latest issue of *Inside Rugby*, the magazine that bills itself as the 'Bible' of the sport Down Under. Apart from the usual retrospective of the 1989 tour – 'the dirtiest ever' – there was a 'where are they now' look at the personnel of twelve years previously in which we learned that Scotland's 1984 Grand Slam hero Peter Dods 'had a healthy career in England before retiring' and that the Ballymena hooker Steve Smith was 'the solid English centre'. The Gloucester hod carrier Mike Teague was amazingly 'now living the life of a country squire on the family property in the north of England'.

Even if the Gabba Test had finished with six sendings-off, a 100–0 victory for Australia and Graham Henry having a heart attack on the touchline, the match would have always struggled to keep State of Origin off the back – and even front – pages. This manufactured, but traditionally rousing, blood-letting between Queensland and New South Wales has no roots in history – unlike Lancashire and Yorkshire the two states had never been to war – but was cannily marketed and invariably captured a lot of attention. There were more Australian autograph hunters chasing the Queensland wing Wendell Sailor in the Sheraton than the whole of the Lions put together and any chance of the tourists earning headlines larger than half an inch tall disappeared totally when Queensland recruited the 34-year-old former Kangaroo Allan Langer, at a rumoured one-off fee of fifty thousand dollars, for the State of Origin decider. Langer was suddenly big news in Australia; he had, in the words of one league commentator been 'pulled out of semi-retirement in England' which must have made interesting news for Warrington, the Super League club who were currently paying him around two thousand pounds a week to play at scrum-half for them.

While the Lions had Richard Hill, and the Wallabies

George Smith, there was no doubt really over who would be the real key man in the First Test. The South African referee Andre Watson had frightened the Lions management earlier in the tour when he remarked that 'he knew how the Lions played'. This was taken as clear evidence that he had fallen for the chicanery of the likes of Eddie Jones, whereas in fact Watson was simply being complimentary. It was felt that Watson, who refereed the 1999 World Cup final and a magnificent Tri-nations game between Australia and New Zealand in Sydney in 2000, was the right man for the job.

On the morning of the Test the Lions squad held a meeting in their large, reserved room in the Sheraton. Some of the midweek team not involved were struck by the deathly, ominous hush. This was thought to be a good sign. Down the street in the media hotel I could detect a few bad signs; one or two British journalists, tired of the alleged cavalier treatment by players and management, half-praying for a Wallabies win – and the chance of some redress.

HACKED OFF

W hen the British and Irish Lions toured South Africa in 1955, their deeds were chronicled by two Welsh, journalists with a writer from the *Daily Mail* joining the party just before the First Test. It was reported that all three became friends for life with most of the players and were treated as an integral part of the party, equals almost. They went sightseeing with the players, played golf with them, dined with them and got drunk with them. They were allowed into the dressing room before and after every match to congratulate or to console. Not surprisingly any marital infidelities, escapades involving too much alcohol or stand-up fights among the travelling players and management went unreported, although incidents certainly happened. In those days, too, the deeds of the Lions had only a peripheral place in the psyche of the British sporting public and media interest was commensurately minimal. Even as recently as 1989, journalists who followed the Australia tour could have been comfortably contained in a Renault people carrier; and the coach Ian McGeechan, while believing that most of the travelling scribes were, in his own words, 'rugby illiterate', could at least sleep easily at night in the knowledge that no microphones were secreted under players' beds or telephoto lenses trained at windows. Times have changed, as Lawrence Dallaglio and the editor of the *News of the World* would be the first to confirm. The private lives of players earning up to thirty thousand pounds a year and happily building high profiles on TV, radio and in newspapers moved into 'the public interest', as the tabloids like to put it, in justification for what anyone else would consider devious practice. Rugby players were suddenly on a par with minor soap stars and Premier League footballers and newspaper editors became interested in who they were sleeping with, what car they were driving, what they ate for lunch and where they went on holiday. Any minor misdemeanours, such as drink driving or failing to pay the council tax, were front-page news.

In Australia, in 2001, however, it became obvious early on that most of the Lions players, with one or two notable exceptions, were horribly un-newsworthy and without much original to say either about themselves or the tour. The players you would have chosen to go out for a chinwag and share a few pints with were the senior ones whose careers had bridged the amateur and professional eras. In other words the old soldiers, like Dai Young and Jason Leonard who still regarded touring as fun; they were paid to play, but essentially still behaved like amateurs. Even Keith Wood, reportedly the life and soul of the party in South Africa in 1997, was taking his responsibilities very seriously in his capacity as Johnson's trusted deputy. Those looking for a wisecrack or two had to look elsewhere, usually in the direction of Rob Henderson.

The blandness of the remainder was perhaps best personified by the man recognised as the 'ultimate professional', Richard Hill. No one could ever attempt to deny that Hill was one of the key men for the Lions and a very nice man, but his public utterances were cerebrally on a par with those of a David Beckham or a Michael Owen. Even his nickname, 'Hilly', spoke volumes for his sheer ordinariness. Jonny Wilkinson may have won the universal vote for the boy you would most like your daughter to bring home for supper, but dragging a quote out of him was as unrewarding and frustrating as that of the man in mythology condemned to roll a stone uphill with his nose. The story of Jason Robinson's past as a drunken gadabout who saw the light and now served Him had been done to death, as had the fact that Tom Smith had epilepsy and Austin Healey asthma. After you had heard a few dozen times that a Lions tour was 'the ultimate honour in my chosen profession', there wasn't a lot left.

It was also a remarkably incident-free journey round a foreign land, enlivened only by the constant sledging from the Australian Super 12 coaches, the assault on Ronan O'Gara in Sydney and Hill in the Third Test, the occasional citing of a player and the Test win in Brisbane. Even the injuries palled in the end. You can have too much of a bad thing and the news impact of major players like Lawrence Dallaglio and Mike Catt being ruled out and sent home was indisputably lessened by the fact that they had arrived in Australia carrying those injuries in the first place. Their departures seemed inevitable.

The only other incidents which raised the British media from their collective torpor were the revelations from the England scrum-half Matt Dawson that all was not sweetness and light backstage and the outburst in print from Healey on the eve of the final Test. These were definitely stories worth 'following up' as they say in the trade and while we may have tut-tutted about their indiscretions and condemned them as Falangists and even, in our usual hypocritical fashion, have castigated the judgment of the newspapers involved, the emergence of the fifth columnists and the extreme reaction of the Lions management – Henry is said to have battered the counter on reception at the Manly Pacific Hotel when he learned of Healey's article in the *Guardian* – undeniably brightened a few dull news days. There can be nothing more boring both to editors and public of simple win or lose match reports, after-game quotes and an inedible diet of reports from the treatment room. Nor was there much salvation for the sensation-hungry, as we shall see, in the official Lions press conferences.

One of the means of overcoming the inaccessibility of the players was to get them to contribute their own views to newspapers and of the thirty-seven players on tour, twenty-five or more were doubling as newspaper or website 'columnists'. In other words, various publications were prepared to pay up to five hundred pounds per item for their exclusive views on what was happening on the field and, very occasionally, off it. As professionals the players were simply 'maximising their earnings potential' as their agents would put it in modern corporate-speak. This, nevertheless, sat uneasily with the management and Lenihan admitted later he would have liked a ban on players' newspaper columns. Unfortunately for him, that was legally impossible as most had signed the newspaper contracts before the Lions one and any subsequent ban may have led to litigation. As Henry was collaborating in a book and contributing his thoughts to a Sunday newspaper you could also say there were precedents in high places. Some half a dozen players were also planning either books on the tour or adding chapters in books to already half-finished autobiographies. There was nothing new in this, although some pundits were later to put the ancillary commercial activities of player-scribes as one of the contributory causes to the eventual series defeat. Books about the doings of the Lions date back to Gubby Allen's account of the 1930 tour while those who castigated Henry must have forgotten the classics by the 1997 manager Fran Cotton (*My Pride of Lions*) and coach Ian McGeechan (*Heroes All*). There was also a *Lions Diary* (author J Guscott), *The Lions Raw* (M Johnson) and *The Lions Uncaged* (J Bentley). These, however, were remarkably free of controversy, the only contentious items appearing in Johnson's book with his rant about the ethics and sanity of the press. He found it extremely difficult to get a decent book review after that.

Among the 2001 'authors' were Johnson – again – Dai Young, Jonny Wilkinson and Jason Leonard. Their books were considered fairly safe bets not to require intense examination by a libel lawyer; Austin Healey's was definitely not. The working titles of the Young and Healey tomes – *The Young One, the Life of a Rugby Legend* and *Foot in Mouth* – just about say everything about the comparative content and respective target audiences. The tour committee had originally wanted to insert a clause in the players' contracts demanding good behaviour and that three thousand pounds be withheld on this understanding. But the players, via their agents, informed Lenihan that they were adults and could be trusted not to wreck hotel rooms, get drunk on the afternoon of a match or lay waste to the local virgin populace. Implicit in this unwritten agreement, however, was that they could also be relied upon to keep to themselves whatever was, or was not, happening behind the curtains. In the end Lenihan agreed, with the proviso that nothing derogatory about the tour be published until thirty days after arriving back in Britain, four weeks that for Lenihan, Henry, Andy Robinson and the rest must have begun ticking like a time bomb.

The players, of course, did not write their columns themselves; their words were ghosted by the rugby writer of whichever newspaper had signed them up. This caused a number of hiccups, mainly because the players were either busy training or busy recovering from training and could spare little more than a snatched five minutes or so before the next line-out drill or session on the treatment table. Unsurprisingly then, most of the bylined stuff was totally vapid and covered events like 'played a round of golf with Pezza and shot under 100 today' to the state of the Manly weather. All of them, with one notorious exception, were ghosted columns; in other words the player spoke his thoughts out loud to a journalist working for whatever newspaper had signed them up and the journalist then retired to his hotel room to add a few flourishes of his own. This was not as easy as it sounds. First, the journalist had to find the player in question, dragging him protestingly away from the table tennis or hotel spa and then coax him into saying something reasonably original. It also involved translating uncoordinated ramblings into readable prose, and putting a metaphorical pen through any repetitive elements. Invariably the long-suffering journalist would also be faced with the task of expanding a snatched conversation in an hotel lobby into something that would fill twenty-four single-column inches of newspaper space.

Thus, a player who offered his opinion that 'we did well in the set pieces' might find it translated in print as 'Australia captain John Eales, one of the world's great line-out forwards let's not forget, never got a sniff against Danny and Johnno and looked a spent force by the time he was subbed in the second half'.

Finally, the precious cargo would be dispatched via a telephone line and laptop modem to the newspaper's head office where it would be trimmed, corrected for spelling mistakes, tagged with a headline and then passed on to a waiting world. To the Lion's management's delight the printed results varied from the bland to the totally unreadable, with the two aforementioned exceptions, the columns carrying the bylines of Dawson and Healey. Dawson's contributions for the *Daily Telegraph* were remarkable not only for their frank content but also that they were written – usually in longhand on hotel stationery – by the player himself. Admittedly, Dawson didn't have to pay much attention to syntax because they were written in terse diary format 'Scrum training and line-outs a.m. Tired again. Slept well' – but they were intelligent and very readable. Dawson's independence of spirit, however, did remove the players' traditional escape clause when faced by the wrath of an offended management: that of 'being misquoted' or 'taken out of context'. Dawson's revelations, on the eve of the First Test, that most of the players were sick of the harsh training regime and that Henry, as some had already suspected, was a pretty uninspiring Lions coach, was badly timed to say the least but at least he was being honest. And it could have been a lot worse – Mick Cleary, the *Telegraph* rugby writer who keyed in Dawson's jottings on his computer and transmitted them to London, had actually toned the original down.

For those of us without a pet player, life was somewhat more difficult and as approaches to them could be made only via the management, in the shape of Alex Broun, most news reports sent back home were either free of the chatty sort of gossip that had characterised previous tours or even, in many cases, outright news. The sort of group interviews offered were not much help, because we all needed the 'personal angle'. Most of the Scottish journalists, for example, couldn't have given a fig about Tom Smith's opinion of his new club, Northampton – unlike the gentleman from that town's evening newspaper – but we were certainly interested in how a Lions tour would improve his Scotland form. The Sundays needed something different from the dailies, the evenings something different from the Sundays and every radio station had to come up with something unique to them. Little wonder the players never looked forward to media days, involving as it did the same old question asked by two dozen different people.

The 2001 Lions tour was accompanied by an unprecedented one hundred-strong army of pressmen of all nationalities, shapes and sizes and ranging in age from nineteen-year-old Sarah Mockford, who had wangled her way on tour as part of her City University course, to seventy-eight-year-old Terry O'Connor, the self-styled doyen of rugby writers. There was the leprechaun-like Barry Coughlan of the *Cork Examiner*, a man who probably weighed as much as one of Martin Johnson's legs and Tony Roche of *the Sun*, who was over 20 stones and with a personality to match. There were radio journalists, website contributors, Sunday newspaper writers, daily newspaper writers, magazine editors and various ghost writers, the most high profile of whom was the towering Nick Bishop, the man charged with producing Graham Henry's tour book. There were widely disparate personalities ranging from the mannered David Hands of *The Times* to his *News International* stablemate, Stephen Jones, the Evelyn Waugh of rugby journalism whose trenchant opinions in the *Sunday Times* had won him an audience that stretched as far as Australia. Indeed, while I never once saw an interview with a Lions player penned by an Australian journalist, Jones and his views were never out of the home newspapers. They relished his insults and such

Right Flying tonight: Tom Smith, right, and Phil Vickery give Danny Grewcock a lift as Robinson and Henry look on

Below Kitten cat: the Lions fans came in all shapes and sizes

Above Lest we forget: the Lions pay silent tribute to baggage master Anton Toia at Coffs Harbour

Left Irish sighs: Lions manager Donal Lenihan often seemed uneasy in the media glare

Welcome aboard: Johnson greets Scott Gibbs as the Welshman arrives as a replacement

Prop the question: Tom Smith gets another grilling. The author, third right, waits his turn

Centre of attention: O'Driscoll in the media spotlight again

The A team: Alex Broun, centre, commiserates as the Lions troop off at Gosford after defeat by Australia A

Above In at the deep end: Austin Healey attempts to keep his head above water in the Manly surf

Right On the ball: Martin Johnson in a rare moment of relaxation on Manly beach

Above Feeling the strain: the pressures on Henry were obvious at times

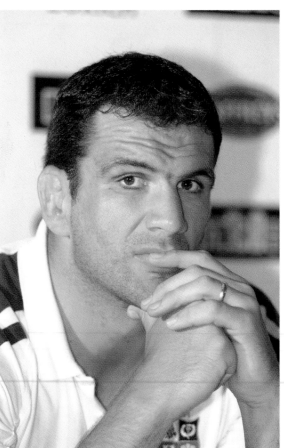

Left Questions, questions: captain Martin Johnson goes through the ordeal of another press conference

Doctor's orders: James Robson, here tending to Brian O'Driscoll in the Second Test, was the busiest man on tour

Watch this space: Jonny Wilkinson lines up in defence in the Third Test

Pride of the Lions: the travelling fans did the tourists – and the Australian economy – proud

Whizz kid: Joe Roff discovers why Jason Robinson's nickname is Billy Whizz at the start of the First Test

Above Must try harder: Scott Quinnell enjoys a crack with Matt Burke and Nathan Grey after his touchdown in the First Test

Right Upwardly mobile: Jason Robinson takes another call. Robinson was one of the Lions success stories

Wounded warrior: Lawrence Dallaglio's injury-ridden tour had far-reaching consequences

Reach for the sky: the roof fell in on the Lions in the Second Test at Melbourne's Colonial Stadium

Barmy Army: the Lions fans lay down a sea of red in Melbourne

Pointing the way: Martin Johnson, pictured during the Second Test in Melbourne, was an inspirational leader

Above Back in the game: Danny
Grewcock, left, celebrates as referee
Jonathan Caplan signals a try for
Neil Back in the Second Test

Left Sheer agony: Rob Howley
realises his tour is over in the
Second Test

Water sport: Johnson takes some light refreshment during training at Manly

Nil returns: Test outcasts Malcolm O'Kelly, left, and Scott Murray work out if their boomerang will come back

Left We have lift off: Lawrence Dallaglio soars in line-out practice, but was there an Aussie spy in the background?

Below Over and out: Jason Robinson, Donal Lenihan, Phil Larder, Graham Henry and assorted hangers-on watch as the Wallabies celebrate the series victory

Right Prize guy: Wallabies flanker George Smith celebrates with the Tom Richards Trophy in Sydney

Left Tears for souvenirs: Brian O'Driscoll tries to come to terms with defeat in Stadium Australia

Left Over and out: Keith Wood
consoles Rob Henderson, left, and
Phil Vickery after the final whistle
in Stadium Australia

Below Sitting targets: Graham
Henry and his assistant coach
Andy Robinson had to dodge most
of the flak for the Lions' failure

was his authority that he even had a column in the Test Match programmes.

The lifestyles of the journos (as they are know in Australia) varied enormously, too. There were some who went for a run every morning and others who never surfaced before noon; there were some who made it their business to join a local gym in every city they visited and those who never left the hotel bar, except to go to an occasional rugby match. There were some who could be considered moderately fit for their profession, including the George Plimpton of British sportswriting, Ian Stafford of the *Mail on Sunday* who had bravely played guested at rugby league with Wigan Warriors and played football for Everton. There was also the former England full-back Alastair Hignell, who suffered from multiple sclerosis, but who never let his illness interfere with his work or his socialising and the invalided former Welsh captain Gwyn Jones, whose career, and almost his life, had been ended by neck injury. Five minutes in the company of Hignell or Jones were as inspiring as anything seen on any rugby field.

And there were the cliques, exclusive bands of varying sizes the constituent of which depended less on innate friendship and more on the fact that if you are wining and dining with a newspaper rival he is unlikely to steal a march by unearthing a story you had missed. As the most famous freemason in the world once famously said: keep your friends close, your enemies even closer. There were the golf cliques, the jogging cliques, the sightseeing cliques, the photographer cliques, the Radio 5 Live clique and the Sky television clique. There were airport taxi-sharing cliques and even a Sydney Opera House-going clique. The Irish went around together in one fast-talking, entertaining bunch, the Scots (all two of them) seldom left each other's side while the English press formed a masonic band of brotherly love, faith and occasional charity of their own.

And there were the Welsh. A nation traditionally prone to homesickness, when abroad such was their fear of the great

101

open spaces of Australia that the Welsh journalists on tour seldom left each other's side. One group of six wandered round – invariably chattering away in their native tongue – like the traditional New Zealand rugby pack: at any stage of the tour you could have thrown a blanket over all of them. On one memorable internal flight to Melbourne, when the unsuspecting Qantas air hostess asked 'Mr Jones to make himself known to the cabin crew by pressing his call button', the interior of the aircraft lit up like a Christmas tree and in Brisbane a rumour swept the tour party that one of the Welshmen had spent three thousand dollars on a prostitute. It seemed an awful lot of dollars until someone pointed out that, divided by six, it was almost a bargain.

Where everyone went their different ways was in the business of a working day and here the time difference between Great Britain and Australia was a boon. In the relatively simple matter of reporting matches the evening kick-offs could not have been better timed. A 7p.m. start in Australia was 10a.m. back home, ample time for the golden prose to be formulated and flow before an early-evening deadline. The only problem with this was that all sports editors back home invariably believed that six o'clock in the evening in the UK was a good time to telephone their Australia correspondents, who by that time were either sleeping peacefully in their beds, or pestering an unsympathetic hotel barman for one for the road.

The centrepiece of the working day, the event around which all our lives revolved, was the management press conference where we would drop whatever we were eating and drinking and gather to hear what we were allowed to hear via a mixture of Lenihan, Henry and Johnson. These press conferences were like set-piece scrums, almost choreographed in their preamble, content and outcome. You could have set them to music. For a start, the Big Three were never on time, their tardiness ranging from a few minutes to over an hour on some occasions. Now a redundant South Wales steelworker who has saved for three years to go on a Lions tour is hardly likely to show much sympathy for a bunch of free-loading journalists moaning about deadlines, but it must be said that these press conferences were a major source of information for a number of daily writers, notably the evening newspapers who had much more unforgiving deadlines, and the radio media. As the ultimate lament of put-upon workers everywhere goes: we have a job to do, too. The Big Three didn't see it that way. There was never either apology or excuse, the management taking it for granted that journos had nothing better to do with their time than sit in an overheated, crowded hotel suite, eating stale sandwiches and twiddling their thumbs. But eventually Lenihan would lead the way into the room in his business-like fashion followed by Johnson, Henry trailing in self-consciously in the rear, to sit themselves before a table groaning with bottles of mineral water, microphones and tape recorders. In front of the table would crouch two or three sound recordists twiddling with buttons while to one side, or at the rear of the room, were a battery of TV cameras. The exception were the Aussie television crews who simply set up their tripods and cameras at the front of the room much to the consternation and disgust of everyone else behind.

The newspaper heavies, the ones used to getting answers to the big questions, would sit in the front two rows with the rest of us stacked in gradual lessening importance and seniority towards the rear seats. Lenihan would sit there twiddling a pencil, Henry pouring a glass of water and Johnson, the angst-ridden giant, knotting his eyebrows with mind focused on some distant battle. Broun, the media relations officer, introduced them individually as if we were meeting for the first time and then ask: 'Any questions?' There would follow thirty seconds of silence with the inde-finable, and almost thrilling, fear that no one would ever actually say anything and management and press would sit facing each other in silence for twenty minutes. Eventually someone would pluck up the courage to say to Lenihan:

'Donal, can you bring us up to date with the injuries?', a signal for the manager to reach into his back pocket for his little black book – a prop as essential and endearing as Charlie Chaplin's cane – and read out the casualty list. Some of the questioning was startlingly mundane, on a par with the Mike Gatting Nose press conference. For those who haven't seen the *Sunday Times* TV advert this features newsreel footage of the former England cricket captain arriving back from the West Indies with a broken nose and two black eyes having been felled by a Malcolm Marshall bouncer. At a subsequent press conference he then describes what happened, finishing with the inevitable news: 'And it hit me on the nose'. To which an earnest hack asked: 'Whereabouts on the nose?'

Lions press conferences, in terms of intelligent probing, were not much better – on the lines of: 'Martin, how important is it to win this series?' or 'Graham, how important is it to win the First Test?' The Aussie media, to Lenihan's undisguised displeasure, would always bring up the violence of 1989 or attempt to stir things up in their inimitable fashion while attempts by the British press to insert some contentious questions into the proceedings were greeted tartly, and with a withering look, by Henry, almost as if saying: 'I won't forget your face, mate.' And always, usually towards the end of the session, a plaintive Welsh voice from the back of the room: 'Grrr-aham, how come Neil Jenkins is not in the team for Saturday?'

None of the Big Three appeared comfortable in the media spotlight or ever bothered to hide their feeling that this was a part of the job they could definitely do without. Lenihan was consumed by an almost missionary zeal to keep players and press apart, telling me during one illuminating interview in Manly: 'Remember that times in rugby change. I always use the analogy of soccer. Alex Ferguson wouldn't allow the media to his training, and I foresee the time, maybe in about four years, when no press will be allowed into rugby training. There are over one hundred accredited media here, and their demands have to be balanced with our need for privacy, as everyone knows the Australians are watching every move we make. In many ways this was virgin territory with the amount of press involved – there has never been such media interest. But in the end it is not my job to come back home the most popular manager ever with the media, having lost a series.'

To other criticisms that the players had been worked far too hard, and that training ground injuries may have been a symptom of that, Lenihan was unsympathetic: 'It's their job; they are professionals. Given a choice between seeing Sydney Harbour Bridge and beating Australia, there is no argument. I remember in 1989 there was this great debate about whether we should go for a day out on the Great Barrier Reef. This time there is not the time: there is too much work to do There is a different attitude now from players and management from the past. Even James Robson, who was the doctor in South Africa four years ago, has remarked on the change. In playing terms, when you look at the old videos it's quite awesome to see the change, even from my day – I get a bit embarrassed when boys these days see us play. Players from my generation would have welcomed the opportunity to see how much better they could have got under the same circumstances as the players of today, not just for the money involved. We got different things out of the game. In the old days, we were the ambassadors, but this time we are here to win. Winning is the satisfaction, not sightseeing. Much of what makes a successful side is common in any era, but there was a special bond in 1989. It just evolved naturally. This time we have worked hard on it.'

It became obvious early on that relations with the press came at the bottom of the list of management priorities. The golden, happy days at Tylney Hall soon gave way to a policy of non-co-operation and occasional subterfuge, particularly over the injuries. After the Second Test in Melbourne where the Lions sustained a number of casualties, Lenihan advised

105

Alex Broun to switch off his mobile phone. The training sessions at Perth and Townsville set the standard for what was to come. Cameras – with the exception of the 'official' snapper from Allsport – were allowed for the stretching and the initial warm-up, but banned for the main business of the day. Not surprisingly, this caused a lot of muttering among the other photographers, most of whose living depended on getting something better than pictures of Jason Leonard attempting to touch his toes. Andy Robinson had an almost paranoid desire for secrecy, a phobia that intensified when the New South Wales assistant coach was spotted as the Lions ran through another series of drills. The travelling press, presumably guilty by some sort of distant association, were banned from the major training sessions from then on.

These were to be conducted, as they laughably called it, 'behind closed doors'. No one pointed out to the Lions management that the training areas invariably were in the middle of a vast open space and overlooked by half a dozen tower blocks from which even the most amateur of Australian spies could have filmed the entire session. In fact, by the time the Second Test came round, the Wallabies knew every single Lions line-out call, their jumpers moving up and down the Lions line as if guided by remote control. Wood, the thrower, confirmed the suspicion when he said: 'We suspected they had cracked the code. I had a couple of errant throws – only a couple – but they seemed to be in position for the throw before we were.' It was another small, but vital, difference between the two sides and again showed that the Aussies were the cutest operators in world sport.

Broun, before declining into the cynicism and in-house gossip that characterised the rest of us, did his best to bridge the unbridgeable gap. As media manager he was in an unenviable position, having to second-guess the whims and variabilities of the management and also pander to more than one hundred story-hungry journalists. At Sydney, on the day after the defeat by Australia A in Gosford, he had arranged an elaborate media day in the Manly Pacific. This was to take place on the first floor of the hotel which had been given over exclusively to the Lions party. They had their own dining area overlooking the seafront, a relaxation and games area featuring a table tennis table and a large television and a separate room stacked with the NTL laptop computers from where they could e-mail home. Close by were a number of large rooms used for the press conferences. It was in many ways an ideal environment, but Broun and others were soon to discover the truth of the old sporting equation: defeat spells surly silence.

One of the main tour sponsors, adidas, had discovered the truth of this earlier on that Wednesday when they had organised a beach day for the press and Lions at Fairweather, close by Manly. There were attractive girls handing out freebies, a barbie, beach rugby and surfing lessons. The weather was glorious and the surroundings idyllic; the only thing missing were the Lions. No one turned up. Among the guests were the 1989 tour manager Clive Rowlands and his wife, and he was totally baffled by this sort of behaviour. He told a story about an occasion earlier in the week when one of the Lions fans had approached Stephen Larkham and asked if he would sign a replica jersey. Larkham had not only signed but had disappeared into the team room and come out with the jersey covered in the signature of every member of the Wallabies party. Rowlands also revealed that ten years after the last Lions tour of Australia he, and most of the players, still had a host of friends in Australia, addling pointedly: 'I wonder how many of these current players will be able to say that in ten years' time?'

Back at the hotel, Broun had valiantly arranged 22 tables with cards bearing the names of individual Lions players on top and there were bottles of water for them and seats opposite for the press. As usual, we had to nominate a player for interview and, in an effort to be more cosmopolitan, I had gone for David Young (to ask him about 1989 naturally), on the basis that you can have too many interviews with Tom Smith. With the exception of Lawrence Dallaglio and a couple of others, no one showed. We waited for an hour and a half and then gave up. Going back down the stairs to reception, a puzzled Iain Balshaw sauntered out of the games room to ask Broun where 'the two guys who want to interview me' were. Broun replied: 'They've all gone to the opera, mate.'

The deliberate distancing of Lions and management from the travelling press caused a lot of frustration and had its negative effects. It is also indisputable that with careful thought the Lions could have used the British media in a positive fashion, if only to answer the propagandists on the Australian side. This was nowhere more apparent than after the Second Test when the Lions were seething over a Nathan Grey 'tackle' which took Richard Hill out of the match and the series. On the Sunday night after the defeat Lenihan complained about Grey's tackle, saying he was 'very unhappy' at the manner in which Hill became injured. Lenihan's statement, however, was quickly submerged by the Wallaby riposte with a number of their former players and journalists accusing the Lions of adopting a dangerous and illegal campaign to wipe out Larkham. This was classic spin-doctoring because although Larkham did receive three late tackles which were penalised, he had carried the arm injury into the match. That did not stop the former Wallaby captain, and Channel 7 television commentator, Simon Poidevin saying: 'Too many times during the Test Stephen Larkham was unfairly targeted, and it was obvious that the Lions were trying to wipe him out. On three occasions the tackles on Larkham were illegal, revolving around high charges or shoulder charges. Early on, Larkham was legitimately hurt during a tackle, but after that it was clear the Lions were deliberately after the winged bird.'

Macqueen was also asked for his views on his favourite

'winged bird' and simply said diplomatically: 'I don't want to make any comment on that at all. I just want to worry about the game. It is an important game and we need to concentrate.' Again, as so often in the past, Macqueen did not need to comment – someone else had done it for him.

From the start of the tour, the tour management were slow to respond to the propaganda war waged by the local press and, of course like schoolyard bullies this only encouraged them even more. So, if the Wallabies had fears about certain aspects of the Lions play there would be stories accusing the Lions of illegality. When Austin Healey complained about sledging from an Australian forward during the match against Queensland, the Australian newspapers were full next day of Michael Foley denying it implicitly and suggesting that the Lions were nothing but a bunch of fibbers. The Lions management never did reply in kind. Most of the propaganda, in fact, came from players, with the management unwilling to dirty their hands in the manner of Dwyer and Jones. The Lions were beaten off the pitch, as well as on it.

After the no-show of the Lions players at Manly there was only one thing to do and I took the spectacular night ferry from Coffs Harbour into Sydney – free of charge because the staff were on strike – to meet a few friends from Edinburgh working on the *Sydney Morning Herald* and to moan about the lot of a touring journalist. The evening passed in time-honoured fashion with a tour of a few pubs, before heading for the Beef and Bourbon, where the Australian Test cricketer Ricky Ponting had once famously floored a transvestite. The final port of call was Baron's Boozer, an all-night, Soho-style drinking den done up like someone's living room, near Kings Cross. There was more drinking, and even some desultory, uncoordinated dancing. Someone passed a strange-smelling cigarette around and suddenly, through the befuddling haze, loomed a familiar figure – Colin Charvis, the Lions flanker. Charvis was not playing that week and any Lions curfew did not apply, but he was in a talkative mood. Unfortunately, for the life of me I can't remember much about the conversation, although one thing did stick in my mind, the moment when he said: 'The back row was picked months ago, before we came out, and there's nothing I can do will change it.' He seemed severely disenchanted, but it was still reassuring to see a human side to a professional rugby player, Outside, there were more non-playing Lions. By way of introducing himself Malcolm O'Kelly grabbed me in a headlock, extremely painful but bearable because finally it signalled that I was one of the boys. I climbed into a taxi to find Phil Greening, Jason Leonard and Rob Henderson there; it was all getting a bit unreal. The rest of the night passed in a glorious daze. I can vaguely recall Henderson, although naturally it was 'Hendo' by now, singing the whole of the *Soldier's Song* in gaelic – not bad for a lad born in Dover – and he and Leonard losing at blackjack in the Star City Casino. Finally, all mates together, and at around six o'clock in the morning, we shared another taxi back to Manly, my new mate Hendo in the back seat and my other new mate Jase in the front and me half-dozing contentedly between; this was what Lions tours were all about. Three miles from Manly I asked the driver to stop while I got out to relieve myself and staggered into some undergrowth, out of sight of the road, that defined the bottom of someone's garden. When I returned, the taxi had gone.

Two hours later, after staggering through hotel reception and past the bemused early risers and alarmed staff arriving for their day shift, I sank into the balming embrace of my bed. After five minutes at least it seemed like that the bedside telephone rang. It was Alex Broun: David Young would see me now.

The justification for virtually anything was victory in the series. No one would care a jot about the inconveniences suffered by a few disaffected journalists if the Wallabies were beaten. The risk was that if the Lions failed, there would be, in the wise words of Brendan Fanning of the *Irish Sunday Independent*, an 'orderly queue of journos waiting to stick the boot in'. There were many who would unarguably have relished the prospect, but after the Gabba they were going to have to bide their time.

On the morning of the match the Lions did receive some encouragement: David Campese's forecast that the Wallabies would win by ten points. If Campese thought that, then we must have a chance, although most of the money was on an Australian victory. The atmosphere at the Wooloongabba cricket ground – the Gabba – was, according to Graham Henry in his newspaper column, 'incredible'. We had to take his word for it because most of the travelling press, in the manner of Adolf Eichmann, were trapped in a totally soundproof glass box normally used by cricket writers, for whom the noise of leather on willow is an intrusion into their slumbers. With the absence of sound effects we had to improvise by turning on the overhead television as loud as possible. Brisbane certainly put on a show with pre-match entertainment of the highest order, but the most startling thing about the preliminaries was the vast sea of red that was the Lions support and the noise they made (at least it sounded incredible relayed second-hand from Channel 7). Johnson, after he had gone outside for the toss, had returned to tell his players that it would be like a home game and the sponsors, with that vision of fifteen thousand fans in replica jerseys and all bearing the NTL logo, must have been besides themselves with glee. There was another lift when the legendary Lion McBride walked in to hand out jerseys. This had always been a special moment for a Lions player and McBride also produced the right, stirring words.

The Lions came out stripped for action, the Wallabies in their tracksuits, but the hosts were leaving nothing else to chance with a message from various of their sporting heroes on the big screen, along with the flickering reminders of Ballymore '89. They had also decided that two anthems would not go amiss and everyone stood for *Advance Australia Fair* and then *Waltzing Matilda*. The latter was sung by a refugee from *Play School* with acoustic guitar and mouth organ, as the Lions stood around with their arms around each other trying to look fierce but respectful. The business of the anthems seemed blatantly loaded. Perhaps the Lions tour committee should follow the example set by Ireland and employ a professional songwriter to write a number of their own. In the good old days every Irish international featured three rousing choruses of *Amhrán na bhFiann, The Soldier's Song* and while the cameras panned down the line in traditional fashion the men from the Republic of Ireland would sing: 'In Erin's cause, come woe or weal; "Mid cannons" roar and rifles peal, we'll chant a soldier's song' while the two token Ulstermen stood grim-faced and with mouths clamped tightly shut at the end. Not surprisingly, come the peace process, this was thought non-politically correct and someone wrote *Ireland's Call* a harmless, non-contentious, little ditty which everyone could join in with. Surely something similar could be done for the Lions?

The men in red, as it turned out, didn't need a rousing battle song for the world champion Wallabies were not so much beaten as totally dismantled by some of the most inspired offence and suffocating defence ever seen on foreign soil. The tourists scored four tries to two and their awesome defence was breached only when down to fourteen men for ten minutes late in the second half. If they had scored forty points, no one would have been surprised. Australia were a poor second best in every department. Their line-out was an embarrassing shambles throughout – they obviously hadn't cracked the Lions codes by then – losing six of their own throws to Johnson and Danny Grewcock and the sight of the great Eales, a marginal figure throughout, trooping off after being substituted in the second half said everything there was to say about Australian rugby on the night. Richard Hill made an awful mess of the reputation of George Smith while Scott Quinnell and Martin Corry totally eclipsed Toutai Kefu and Owen Finegan in the other back-row battle. But it was the Wallabies' much-vaunted midfield that proved their real Achilles heel, with the Irish centre partnership of Brian O'Driscoll and Rob Henderson carving them open at will. For the great Daniel Herbert and his partner Nathan Grey, in particular, it was a match to forget. It was, however, far from perfect. As against Queensland a fortnight earlier, the tourists stood off and watched in the second half, and gave away far too many penalties. But the Aussies had been mugged in spectacular style and couldn't even dredge up the time-honoured whinge about the Lions' strong-arm tactics. It was a squeaky clean contest throughout.

For Macqueen, there were also concerns about Larkham, who went off with a damaged elbow and the Australians also lost their first-choice hooker Jeremy Paul after a serious injury left him with medial ligament damage. At the time it looked all up for the Wallabies.

While admitting that he was one of the game's most exciting runners, there had been concerns about Robinson and his rugby league habit of turning infield when in possession, for getting tackled into touch in league is a crime punishable by death in that sport. Naturally, Robinson proceeded to scoot over with an outside jink after just three minutes from his first touch in a Lions test. So much for the pundits. And so much for coaching because no training in the world could have produced that sort of speed and precision. It all happened when O'Driscoll left Grey floundering and Quinnell and full-back Matt Perry manufactured the opening for Robinson. Given a one on one against the cumbersome full-back, Chris Latham, it was no contest. Latham looked infield, Robinson went the other way and the Lions were ahead. The unbiased British pressmen rose as one in their sweaty glass box to bawl: 'Yuu-uu-s!'

Wilkinson missed the difficult conversion, but the Lions

113

had made a devastating statement of intent, and the home nervousness was obvious as the hapless Latham dropped a lofted ball from Rob Howley, hooker Jeremy Paul hung on in the tackle and Wilkinson was just short with the penalty. It was stirring stuff and almost at once Rob Henderson broke through the middle, and although Joe Roff intercepted to boot the ball back into the Lions' 22, Wilkinson and Quinnell combined to take play back towards the Aussie line; and when O'Driscoll kicked ahead, Andrew Walker had to carry over. The Australian scrum was demolished at the resulting set-piece, and when it was re-set, prop Nic Stiles had to resort to the longest bootlace-tying session in rugby history to earn the harassed Wallabies a breather.

The first moment of Australian offence did, however, produce a score when Grewcock came in from side of a ruck after a rush of blood to the head by Dafydd James, the Welshman trying to run the ball out of his own 22. Walker pegged the score back to 5–3 but missed badly after George Smith finally made a trademark turnover and Quinnell failed to stay on his feet, a scenario that was to become familiar as the series wore on. The Lions were winning the physical battle, too, with Grey needing lengthy treatment after a clattering from Keith Wood.

After some great driving work by Johnson and his pack, Eales handled on the ground and Wilkinson's kick landed bizarrely on the top of the upright – a good future one for *A Question of Sport* and 'What Happened Next?' It was Wilkinson's third miss out of three, but it mattered not as O'Driscoll immediately drifted past the ponderous Finegan down the right. Jason Robinson came off the opposite wing in support and James made up for his earlier aberration by crossing in the corner through Latham's poor tackle. Wilkinson this time converted emphatically from wide out.

Up in the box we could scarcely believe our eyes. The half-time score of 12–3 to the Lions seemed minimal reward for forty minutes of total dominance, but the underdogs were not finished and emphatically twisted the knife on the restart. Burke had replaced the ineffectual Latham, but was found just as wanting as O'Driscoll was put straight through the middle by Wilkinson, and the Irishman beat Grey and Paul with relish before consummately sidestepping the replacement full-back for a wonderful try at the posts. At 19–3, the red mass below us was exultant. Wilkinson widened the margin with four minutes of the half gone when the Wallabies' backs went offside after O'Driscoll had cut them to shreds again, and the world champions were in tatters.

On fifty-one minutes, Henderson galloped joyfully through the midfield again, beating Herbert, Grey and Roff in a run to within three metres. Iain Balshaw, the replacement for Perry at full-back, was stopped when he picked up, but Quinnell powered over past Burke from the ruck, nodding emphatically at the downcast Wallabies to signal a try. Wilkinson's conversion made it 29–3, and was a signal for a mass of Macqueen changes with Elton Flatley on for the dispirited Larkham and Michael Foley replacing the stricken Paul.

Flatley at least managed to spark his back-line, and there was a period of home pressure with only a magnificent tackle by Robinson keeping Burke out in the corner, the video referee deciding that he had been forced into touch. The Wallabies, however, were at last finding some rhythm. Kefu got over under the posts, but Foley had obstructed the Lions tackler, and the lack of discipline in Aussie ranks was a sight for (some) sore eyes. With twenty minutes left, Corry was yellow-carded for handling on the ground again, and almost at once Walker found a damaging angle inside Robinson for a try. Burke, however, missed the straight-forward conversion, as he did when Roff's inside pass put Grey through a minute later, and even the sin-binning of Phil Vickery could not persuade anyone that the Australians could mount a recovery.

Such was the measure of the tourists' inability to put a foot wrong that when Wood tried an absurd drop-goal from fully thirty-five metres out, it would have surprised no one if the ball had sailed high between the posts. Wood and the Lions by then were simply taking the mickey.

At the end the golden glitter – planned to celebrate a Wallabies victory – came pouring down from the stands and the metaphors started fluttering around, too, on the lines of 'even the skies wept for the world champion Aussies'. Greg Growden of the *Sydney Morning Herald*, was less romantic. 'Look at that, a golden shower,' he said. At times like this it is hard to remain objective and there was perhaps a vaguely triumphalist air about the British media. But then we had actually managed to beat Australia at something and perhaps some measure of one-eyedness – nothing as extreme as the Aussies, mark you – was forgivable . . . The opening of my match report in *Scotland on Sunday* possibly represented a fairly typical, balanced view: 'World champions? What world champions?'

If the British cocks crowed that night, the 'golden shower' out on the Gabba playing area got the predictable gubbing in the Australian media next day. The consolation for Macqueen was that the Wallabies could surely never play so badly again. He had mistimed their preparation and his team were, in the words of Henry, 'slightly undercooked'. Macqueen informed his team later in the dressing room that although it was a long way back, they could still win the series, and that he would remain faithful with the team that had failed, although Burke would certainly stay at full-back for Chris Latham. Paul was out for the season after rupturing his cruciate and medial knee ligaments and Glenn Panoho had also injured his neck. The casualty list is always longer in a losing side, as the Lions were to discover a week later.

As for the Lions they had pulled all the right strings, even the psychological master stroke of getting McBride to make the pre-match speech and hand out the jerseys. Johnson revealed: 'He told us it would be tough, it would be very painful and there would be times when our bodies would not want to continue, but that we must push ourselves through the pain barrier. He acknowledged that things had changed in rugby since his day but that he knew what we were all going through. He struck just the right chord with the boys.' Johnson, a Lion in the McBride mould, had then asked that his players 'stand up and be counted'. Unfortunately for the Lions one of their number chose to stand up to be quoted.

It was maybe thirty minutes after the match, with the euphoria still rising, that Lenihan went on television and was asked about a diary piece written by Matt Dawson in the *Daily Telegraph* criticising the Lions management and the training regime. As it was the first Lenihan knew about any such article he was naturally dumbfounded. They might as well have shoved him under the cold shower in the Gabba dressing room.

SUN, SEA, SAND AND SEDITION

In the immortal words of Dawson the Diarist in one of his subsequent, more temperate, *Daily Telegraph* pieces: 'No sooner did the final whistle sound than I realised that the shit was going to hit the fan.' Lenihan and Henry were almost besides themselves with rage and there was talk of disciplinary meetings, fines and even that ultimate sanction – escorting the player in disgrace to Brisbane Airport for the next plane home. Dawson had broken the cardinal rule of a player-columnist: say whatever you like within reason, but under no circumstances criticise the management or fellow players. His comments also illustrated the classic conundrum surrounding celebrity rugby columns; journalists complained that the players had nothing to say and then belly-ached when someone – in another newspaper of course – actually came out with something readable. While the editorial top brass at the *Telegraph* basked in their old-fashioned and unlikely scoop the rest of us scrambled into print to condemn the little quisling and recommend all sorts of things ranging from a slap around the head to public disembowelling. All these damning verdicts were issued, unusually for our profession, with the benefit of having all the facts to hand. As the Lions management had discovered, modern communications meant nothing stayed secret for long, even ten thousand miles away. No sooner had the news broken than we all logged on to the Internet to search for telegraph.com and to catch up with Dawson's thought processes. Then we could deliver our own sanctimonious judgments.

As it turned out, Dawson's Diary, until then, had been amusing and entertaining although it didn't take a degree in human psychology to detect a gradual escalation of critical comment. Rewinding events back to departure from

Heathrow, Dawson had remarked in the manner of a school-boy writing his first holiday postcard home: 'Just about packed in time for 8.15 departure for Heathrow. Midday flight to Singapore, 14 hours. Allocated seat next to Graham Henry for flight to Perth. Boys gave me lot of brown nose banter. Never really spoken to GH. Seems v knowledgeable. Enjoys the game. Good analyst. Likes to see flair.'

Fifteen double training sessions later, two moderate per-formances on the field and in the certain knowledge that Rob Howley would be the Test scrum-half, Dawson had done a dramatic about-face and wrote on the Tuesday of the match against Australia A: 'Seems like coaches have forgotten what a long season the boys have had. Yes, we're up for a Lions tour but there's only so much that is good for you. GH does pre-match, but doesn't inspire me at all.'

And after the defeat: 'Donal Lenihan hacked me off with post-match comments. Treated us like kids. As if we wanted to lose. Have flogged us for three weeks. Defeat was waiting to happen. Senior players warned management, but they didn't listen.'

Until then Dawson's bleatings could have been put down simply to sour grapes, the anguished breast-beating of a player who knows his chances of repeating his three Test appearances against South Africa in 1997 were looking distinctly remote. But his entry for the Thursday provided a real bombshell: 'It's official – some of the boys have decided to leave the tour. We said at Tylney that if this should happen we would implement peer pressure, but to be frank, with so many young players it is hard to avoid. No doubt when the Tests are upon us everyone will be fully focused.' This was mind-boggling news; in three weeks, according to Dawson, the tour had deteriorated from the greatest honour in players' lives – as they were so fond of telling us – to something close to a Serbian forced labour camp, good only to abscond from.

Dawson was later to come out with the somewhat lame justification that he meant the 'boys were going to leave the tour mentally', but the damage had been done. It was only later, much later, that other players raised their heads above the parapet to admit in public that Dawson may have had a point. Colin Charvis complained, as he had apparently done to me and drinking companions in Baron's Boozer in Sydney, that there were few opportunities for relaxation or to go sightseeing, that the tour was all training and that anyway the Test team had been pre-selected long before departure. David Young's midweek side, he said, were treated as second-class citizens, there as cannon fodder for the Test side in that they simply impersonated the opposition in training sessions, and that there was no communication with the management. The Scotland hooker Gordon Bulloch was more specific and implied that it was all an Anglo-Saxon plot and they were being flogged in training in a bid to bring the Celts up to speed with the English. He also claimed that the reason he lost his bench place to Dorian West was because the Englishman was familiar with Robinson and Larder's drills, a valid point given the narrow timescale of the tour. Dan Luger and Iain Balshaw also more or less confirmed what Dawson had written. Luger, safely back home in southern England a fortnight after leaving the tour was to describe life with the Lions as 'black and tortuous' and he added: 'Daws was right – Graham Henry has trained us to a standstill. My legs have never been so tired, even in pre-season training, but that is Henry's decision. He's the man and he simply wants to get the job done. Lions teams of the past always had a great party off the field – win or lose – but that has vanished. The social side of touring now is almost non-existent. We don't need to party – but we do need to relax and maybe the management have not given enough thought to that.'

Balshaw moaned piteously about not being used correctly, as if the whole Lions game plan should have been designed around him. He said: 'England use me wide out, but the Lions expected me to run into traffic in midfield. I am definitely not a crash ball runner.' But Balshaw also made a more balanced point when he added: 'The social side was nowhere near as team-based as it looked on the *Living With The Lions* video from the last tour. There were obviously groups doing social activities but we didn't really do anything as a team. I think that if we had done more of that sort of thing then we may have seen a different attitude in the camp.'

In the light of all this substantiation perhaps Dawson should have taken legal advice and gone to court to have his fine repaid: 'M'lud, we will prove quite conclusively that our client's remarks had justification in fact.'

Dawson's outburst did have another less obvious, more negative, effect – it was immediately picked up by the Australian press and served to take away not only some of the begrudging credit due to the Lions but also some of the maulings which traditionally go the way of Australian sportsmen who have failed miserably, although with Allan Langer and State of Origin in town anything else was going to struggle to get more than a passing mention. Another whingeing Pom, however, was good news in any language.

The Lions couldn't afford to send Dawson packing. As back-up to Howley he was almost irreplaceable, particularly as Henry plainly saw Healey in a No 9 shirt only in the direst emergency and this wasn't one. On the way back to the Brisbane Sheraton from the Gabba, like any sensible professional player, Dawson formulated a plan of action – with his agent. They decided that a little contrition would not go amiss. Like a drunk who has made a complete ass of himself in company the evening before, Dawson woke up the Sunday morning and after working out that it hadn't all been a bad dream set about doing all the right things. He did the rounds of hotel rooms to see Lenihan, Henry, Robinson and Larder individually and apologised for the timing and the breach of trust and confidence. An unsympathetic Lenihan told him he would be fined; the others were reasonably forgiving. At the team meeting before the flight

121

to Canberra on the Sunday afternoon, Dawson addressed the whole group. He said sorry to his team-mates en masse and his apology was accepted, hardly surprising as half the party felt exactly the same way. Lenihan announced to the press corps, in the manner of team managements every-where when disciplinary matters crop up, that the player 'would be dealt with internally and the matter was closed'. Dawson would not be available for interview and there would be no further comment from player or management. We howled our frustration, to no avail, although in terms of a news story there was some minor consolation with the revelation that Colin Charvis had copped a two-match ban for kneeing Nic Stiles during the Test. Some measure of revenge for the Australians, too.

As so often happens in sport, Dawson was handed the immediate opportunity to make amends – to 'answer his critics' as he bizarrely put it – by being named in the team to face Super 12 champions ACT Brumbies in Canberra. This was to be the final midweek match of the tour and brought the Lions face-to-face with their Australian tormentor-in-chief, Eddie Jones. Fast Eddie, as he was known by then, was fresh from leading the Brumbies to the Super 12 title and was still basking in the afterglow of the Australia A victory. From a journalistic point of view the one thing dreaded above all else was not a Lions defeat, but another victory speech by Jones. A Brumby, we discovered, is Aussie argot for a runaway horse. It can also mean a wild, unruly person.

We arrived in midwinter Canberra on Sunday night to find Australia's capital city closed. It was like being lost in a huge unlit park, with no sign of life, no traffic on the wide boulevards and without even a watering hole. It was Ho Chi Minh City during a curfew. Undeterred, after checking in to the soulless apartment block that was to be our home for three nights, we bravely set forth into a bitter night to find some social life, eventually after much searching coming across an oasis glowing in the dark and a large illuminated sign that announced King O'Malley's Pub. The barman was from Dublin and with a sudden invasion of British and Irish Lions fans he had probably not served so much Guinness since he left McDaid's Bar. He was bribed to put the replay of the Lions match on one of the pub's two televisions and the travelling support happily sat at one end of the bar revelling in the previous night's Test win on one TV set while all the locals sat watching State of Origin III on the other. An occasional loud cheer came from both sides of the great divide.

The re-run of the Lions Test win was not only an opportunity to do some crowing and revel in a stupendous victory, but also the first chance for most of us to discover if what we had produced for that day's newspapers – reports written on the spot and without the benefit of hindsight let's not forget – matched reality. In other words, was it Matt Perry who gave Robinson the scoring pass for the first try, or someone else? It was the moment of truth. It was also the first exposure for many of us to what passes for informed TV commentary in Australia. This was in the hands of Channel 7's Chris Handy, known as 'Buddha' less for his wisdom than the statistic that he weighs around twenty-one stones. Handy is a professional fat man who believes that being that size makes him cuddly and jolly whereas in reality, impartiality and objectivity are foreign concepts to him. But even 'Buddha' found it difficult to find excuses, or blame external factors like the refereeing, weather, dirty play by the Lions or the soulless venue, for Australia's abject display. It was a glorious evening. The consolation for Macqueen and his chastened Wallabies was the fact that their defeat would be lost among other, more important, matters. On the way to the men's room at half-time I passed the 'Australian' TV in time to see Langer stretching over the New South Wales line for a try. Cue another 20-page supplement on 'Alfie' on the Monday morning.

The reunion with Jones and his boys was scheduled for

Bruce Stadium, another purpose-built ground shared by the Brumbies and the Canberra Raiders. It was a breathlessly cold night and most of the journalists sat huddled together for warmth high in the stand. We were suddenly very close, one big, heat-seeking clique and the writers actually filing that night spent most of the time shivering over keyboards or attempting to beat life into numbed fingers. As with every other venue, the pre-match entertainment was out of the top drawer, but with the definite feeling that, like everything else in Australia, it was an opportunity to flog a few things. The cheerleaders were sponsored and before kick-off a platoon of sky divers soared out of the cold night sky to land in the centre circle. This display of skill and daring was diluted somewhat by the sight of the advertising for Joe Bloggs Garage on their parachute canopies. A large screen opposite plugged Bundaberg Rum nonstop throughout the game's eighty minutes and the day cannot be far off in Australia when players will be ordered to stop whatever they are doing on the field for a commercial break.

Like Queensland and New South Wales, the majority of the twelve Wallabies in the ACT – or to give them their correct title the Australian Capital Territories Computer Associates Brumbies – squad had been pulled for various reasons, but they still constituted a formidable line-up. Their captain, Jim Williams, was playing his last match before joining Munster – cue the violins and the stories about 'winning this one for Jim' – and they had also been over in New Zealand on a two-game warm-up tour specifically for the Lions. They had some by now well-known faces, including Justin Harrison who had destroyed the Test hopes of Scott Murray and Malcolm O'Kelly in the Australia A game at Gosford – and managed to get up a lot of Lions' noses – and the brilliant centre, Graeme Bond. They were also fielding the former Leicester centre Pat Howard at stand-off. Howard had been around when the Brumbies were formed, played for them for three years and then

124

headed to the UK to become one of the most influential players in England. The Lions made fourteen changes from their Brisbane starting XV and it didn't escape the notice of many of the selected players that this was probably the last-ever chance to wear the red jersey. Dawson had been nominated as kicker despite the presence of Ronan O'Gara at stand-off and Henry pulled one of his clever little tricks by naming Johnson on the bench in an effort to show support for the much-abused midweek side. Johnson didn't get on, although when the Lions were trailing – quite a lot of the time in this match – he made a point of threatening to, jogging up and down meaningfully in his quilted overalls. The rest of the time he spent glowering from the touchline. But even Johnson didn't seem to be much of a motivating factor as the Brumbies and Jones came within a whisker of achieving the unthinkable, the decisive try for the Lions coming on the last play of the match nearly a minute after the siren. It was hailed as a glorious fightback and undoubtedly it was, but again there was the sense of the distance between the Test team and the midweek 'stiffs' and in the first half in particular the Brumbies cut the Lions much-vaunted defence to ribbons. The fact that the Brumbies were mainly comprised of their regular reserves' bench, and a few new players hoping for a training contract next season, was somehow masked by the drama of the last five minutes. The home side tore into the tourists from the opening whistle, leading 19–3 through tries by wingers Mark Bartholomeusz and Willie Gordon and flanker Des Tuiavii. We could hear Eddie already. Fortunately, the Lions rallied towards the end of the half as the Brumbies began to tire, first kicking a penalty, then scoring an interception try by Austin Healey who snapped up a pass from his former Leicester team-mate Howard and ran the length of the field to the posts, slowing only slightly to look back and offer a few taunts to the cover.

The second half was dominated by the Lions as they visibly picked up their work rate. By the eighty-minute mark they had pegged the Brumbies' lead back to just five points. And then from a passage of play lasting nearly two minutes the Lions pounded the Brumbies tiring defence, Healey eventually scoring out wide to level the scores. For sheer drama it was hard to beat, particularly as bad boy Dawson now had the chance to win the match with his conversion. It was a difficult angle, but such is sport that no-one had the slightest doubt that he would kick it. Dawson grabbed his Lions jersey badge like a Premiership footballer to brandish it at the exultant red army in front of him before being buried under a scrum of grateful team-mates. There was a lot of hugging and kissing. He was forgiven.

Jones appeared alone at the Brumbies press conference, held in a chilly basketball hall, and reminded us that this was in reality his second team, adding: 'I'm pretty proud of the way the guys played. We gave it everything we could; in the end we just couldn't hang on. Justin Harrison has really tormented the Lions in the two matches he's played against them and showed he's a real class player. It was a great exhibition of rugby between two contrasting styles. We're probably noted as a side that is probably more skilful than physical, but we went out there to take them on physically. I think if you can do that then you can use your skills later on in the match. I'm feeling really proud of the guys.' With that Jones was off, after his last appearance as Brumbies coach. The feeling was that he would be around to torment us for years to come.

He was right about Harrison. The towering lock had put himself about in no uncertain manner and seemed to have formed a mutual unappreciation society with Healey. When he scored towards the end of the first half, Harrison pointed out that the Lions were still losing. Healey had said by way of reply: 'That's my first try.' After he touched down to tie the scores at the end of the game he went up to Harrison again to tell him: 'And that's my second.' Not surprisingly, Harrison took great exception and there was a bit of a scuffle with the two players going eyeball to eyeball, or rather Healey eye-balling Harrison's navel. It was all good, clean fun, but was to have unfortunate consequences later. The other Lions whinge of the night was the refereeing of Peter Marshall, which was a disgrace and said everything about Lenihan's fears about the lack of neutral referees. As Willie John McBride put it: 'If you've got a bloke from round the corner refereeing he will always be biased because he has to go back and live round that corner.'

Dawson, the villain-turned-hero, did not appear at the press conference but told his growing army of fans in the *Daily Telegraph* later: 'There was more pressure on that kick than I am able to describe. I truly enjoyed the night and all the challenges it brought, especially after we were down at half-time. I wanted to have a big game to prove critics wrong about what they saw as the reasons for writing the diary. It wasn't because of sour grapes or petulance and there was only one way to show them that wasn't so. The crowd and the squad have given me so much positive chat that it makes you wonder what the papers are making of it all.'

Henry was due to announce his squad of twenty-two for the Second Test on the Wednesday, twenty-four hours after the Brumbies match but instead the Lions pulled a fast one with the announcement of a twenty-seven-strong squad. Lenihan justified this by pointing out that there were a number of injury concerns, including Perry whose groin injury made him doubtful. There were also question marks about the likely replacements. Henry then blithely announced he would name his line-up the day before the Melbourne Test and the Australians and their media naturally saw this as a massive subterfuge. The Lions were playing psychological games – something the Wallabies would never dream of – and there were vague mutterings about invoking IRB laws which stated that a Test squad had to be announced at least forty-eight hours before a match.

At least the initial announcement of twenty-seven names meant there were five fewer long faces and gave us all a lot more interview opportunities. While almost everyone concentrated on the players I sneaked off to grab Steve Black who spoke movingly about Anton Toia's death and how it had effected him. He also revealed his mother was ill with cancer. I wondered where was the shoulder for him to cry on when he needed it. He also surprised me by nodding off in his comfy hotel chair mid-interview. Was it something I said? It turned out he was a virtual insomniac, sometimes getting up at 4a.m. A newspaper interview was as good a time as any to catch up.

The only change for the Second Test was the naming of Neil Back in place of Martin Corry, who had obviously not put his hand up high enough. It meant that Back went to the open-side of the scrum with Richard Hill going to the blindside. Corry moved on to the bench after the suspension of Charvis. Much to the disgust of the Scottish press corps, Bulloch lost his bench place to Dorian West, who had only been with the party for a week. Perry recovered from his groin injury and Balshaw's frown became even more pronounced. Dawson had also recovered from his fine and bollocking and was on the bench for Howley again.

It has to be said that we left Canberra without many regrets. As capital cities go it is hardly in the class of Paris or Vienna and it was also bloody freezing. Melbourne, with its quaint trams, Victorian architecture, mild winter temperatures and views over the Yarra River was more our scene. We were in the Grand Hotel, an amazing establishment with corridors a quarter of a mile long leading from a reception area the size of a bathroom. The corridors stretched almost out of sight and were straight out of Jack Nicholson's holiday hideaway in *The Shining*. There were an interesting couple of days leading up to the Test containing all the best and worst of sports reporting. On the Thursday we had been summoned to a press conference in the Grand by the International Rugby Board, featuring some well-known rubicund faces under the stage management of the former Scotland centre Chris Rea. The session got off to a bad start when the IRB underestimated the size of their potential audience and we had to find a room larger than the broom cupboard originally booked; there was a finger buffet that would have required a miracle of biblical proportions to satisfy the hungry throng and, once we had settled, the IRB chief executive Vernon Pugh announced that there would be an annual match between the northern and southern hemispheres, a sort of all-star game. With the Lions falling apart with injury it seemed somewhat insensitive, but it was already in doubt. Pugh said it would be in June, or July, or November, or December, and it turned out the decision had been made without consultation with Australia and New Zealand, who immediately expressed grave misgivings. Pugh then also announced that someone called Geoff Evans had been appointed to one of the IRB's many committees. The famous words of Carling – something about 'old' and 'farts' – came back and some of the many cynics present wondered out loud why Pugh and his cronies had travelled all the way to Melbourne to tell us that. The answer was obvious and lay just around the corner in the Colonial Stadium. Fortunately for the long-suffering hacks, Zurich then came to the rescue again, hosting a free booze-up in the city's All Stars Sports Cafe, spectacularly sited in the Crown Entertainment Complex on the banks of the Yarra. Even the opening of the First Test at Lord's, and the clunk-clunk of England wickets falling, could not dampen spirits.

The respective teams also prepared for the match in their own ways. On the Thursday some of the Lions did their cultural bit with a visit to Ramsay Street, home of the soap opera *Neighbours* – and once of Alex Broun before he had gone on to greater things. Jonny Wilkinson went for a game of tennis at Melbourne Park, the venue for the Australian Open, while Andy Robinson with his wife and four kids spent a rare day off at the aquarium. The build-up to the game was almost unbelievably sedate, the only minor rush of excitement coming on the Friday when the Wallabies announced that the roof to the Colonial Stadium would be closed for the match. The Lions immediately objected. This was not because they thought it was the wrong decision – rain had been forecast for the Friday and Saturday – but the fact was that if the Wallabies wanted something, we certainly did not.

The atmosphere in the Lions hotel on Saturday was incredible with hundreds of red-jerseyed fans milling around singing and cheering and wishing luck and posing for photographs with players, all of whom obliged with varying degrees of good grace. The travelling support were a remarkable bunch ranging from pensioner couples who had spent their life savings on the trip to blue collar workers from every industrial quarter of the British Isles who had worked constant night and back shifts to raise the money. The inevitable anoraks were there to plague the Lions players – one of them even asked me for my autograph in Manly on the basis 'that if you've shook the hand of Martin Johnson, that's good enough for me' – but the punters, as the press pack somewhat uncharitably knew them, were a marvellous, uplifting bunch and a boon to the Australian economy. Even David Campese, struggling to clear two thousand dollars a day in his Sydney sports shop normally, reported daily takings of up to twenty thousand dollars during the tour.

Crossing the vast overhead walkway leading to the island that is the Colonial Stadium there was hardly a gold shirt in sight. This despite the best efforts of the ARU who after seeing the takeover by Lions fans of the Gabba had desperately handed out hats and scarves in Wallaby colours. Any Wallaby fans spotted were immediately greeted with the chant: 'You're only wearing yellow because it's free!' Inside there was a stadium record crowd of 56,605 and a four-hundred-million TV audience, who happily watched some sumptuous pre-match entertainment including a Welsh male voice choir, Scottish pipe band, Irish dancers and a traditional English brass band. There were green and gold flares by the side of the pitch and on the crossbars and the customary downpour of golden glitter before and after the match. There were numerous tiresome choruses of *Waltzing Matilda*, a recorded goodwill message from Wimbledon finalist Pat Rafter and a demented soul with a microphone who did everything but stick pins in effigies of Martin Johnson and Co in his eagerness to see a home victory.

Meanwhile, the macho stuff was going on in the dressing rooms. Macqueen, who is surprisingly superstitious – he always goes for a sushi meal with his wife Liz before a Test – asked the Wallabies coach of 1984 Alan Jones to address the team. Jones is a well-known sporting maverick and at the time was involved in a libel case involving the rugby league referee Bill Harrigan. But he'd do for Macqueen – simply because the Wallabies beat the Springboks at Colonial Stadium the previous year after Jones had addressed the team. Over in the Lions quarters Lenihan – he had run out of former Lions captains – spoke about the history and tradition of the tourists. Henry did the tactical stuff; Black went round beaming encouragingly at everyone. The smiles, however, soon faded.

The roof at the stadium may have been closed, but it still fell in on the Lions in spectacular style and with a resounding clatter. It was a crushing defeat in the end, but oddly by half-time most of us believed the series was won, even some of the cocky Australian journalists. But an inopportune pass early in the second half from Jonny Wilkinson gave Joe Roff an interception try and suddenly the Wallabies looked like world champions. It was hurtful stuff.

Then there was the physical damage. Wilkinson was carted off to Royal Melbourne Hospital with what looked horribly like a suspected broken leg after taking on Daniel Herbert – Wilkinson seemed to have a big thing about trying to knock over Herbert – once too often. An x-ray later determined that it was heavy bruising but at the time

131

the portents didn't look good. Wilkinson also had company in casualty, Hill, O'Driscoll and Howley also finishing the evening there. Only O'Driscoll was to recover and the Lions were suddenly faced with dipping into the midweek dirt-trackers, the players Henry had told were surplus to his requirements, for replacements.

On the field, the Lions were outscored by three tries to one, George Smith ruled the breakdown once Hill had gone off and the tourists' line-out was reduced to a shambles at times. One week after the First Test the Lions were in a similar position to the Wallabies after that; confidence dented, key players injured and everything to play for.

Initially, the Lions had carried on where they left off in Brisbane, incisive early breaks by James and O'Driscoll shredding the home midfield. But, worryingly, the final passes went astray this time, and the tourists also lost the first two line-outs on their own throw. They went ahead with Wilkinson's first two successful penalties, and although Matt Burke responded with one straight in front of the posts, O'Driscoll then produced a typical moment of wizardry for the opening try. His kick and gather in full flight was ended when he was heavily tackled, but while he was being treated for a neck injury, Wilkinson kicked superbly to the corner where Burke was pushed into touch. Danny Grewcock at once won the line-out and Back was driven over by the pack. But Wilkinson missed a succession of penalties and also dropped a potential scoring pass; and the Wallabies, experts at recognising the swing of a pendulum, responded at once. Johnson was penalised for one of three illegal late tackles on Larkham and Burke narrowed the gap to 11–6. The wheels were falling off; Hill suffered concussion after a blatant elbow in the face from Grey and within a minute Wilkinson committed the fatal error that was to turn the series. Roff had a lot to do and O'Driscoll made a marvellous attempt at a cover tackle at the corner flag, but the video referee took almost no time at all to decide that the try was good. Another Burke penalty took Australia into the lead

132

for the first time in the series at 14–11 and within three minutes Larkham put Roff away down the short side and the wing outfoxed James, Jason Robinson and O'Driscoll for a try close enough to the posts for Burke to make no mistake with the conversion. Wilkinson, in between two misses, did pull the score back to 21–14 when the Lions pack drove relentlessly into the Wallabies 22, but it was apparent that the tourists were attempting to run from deep too often and the Australian cover simply pulverised them. Alarmingly, the Lions' first-time tackles were also proving ineffectual, and, when Owen Finegan lumbered past Henderson, Burke clutched the flanker's lofted pass and took three Lions over the line with him. Two more penalties and the injuries to Wilkinson and Howley capped a miserable night and the golden glitter that rained down was suddenly quite appropriate.

Henry made the right noises about rising from the ashes of Melbourne later, although with the loss of Hill and Howley and the damage to Wilkinson he appeared to be simply going through the motions. 'They have a huge challenge now,' said the coach. 'But I am sure the character in this team will see them handle that challenge. We are basically in the same situation as Australia were last week.' Johnson confirmed what many had suspected: that the Wallabies had done their homework – or something more devious – on their line-out. He said: 'We missed one or two calls, and we also turned over a lot of ball, and that gave the Australians some momentum. They got the points on the board, and from then on just got better and better. We are battered and bruised after a very hard series and a long, hard season, and it is a mental thing now. We need to get our heads up very quickly.'

Being the Lions against the Wallabies, there were also a few bones of contention to chew over after the match. Phil Larder labelled Wallabies centre Grey's tour-ending tackle on Hill as 'a blatant foul' and the Lions anger only increased when the citing commissioner, New Zealander

David Gray, after allegedly poring at great length over the video, decided that Grey had no case to answer. Larder, who had gone through the tour with hardly a public peep out of him, was now roused to say: 'If I go back to my rugby league days, if one of my players had made a tackle like that, then I would have expected him to have been on the sidelines for six weeks. It was a blatant hit with the elbow on the chin, no doubt about it. I was very, very disappointed. Nathan Grey, I feel, is a fairly clean player who acted out of character, but it was a blatant foul. We've looked at it frame by frame, and he comes across and hits Hilly with his elbow. He hits him on the point of the jaw, Richard went straight down and was out for the count. To me, that is not part and parcel of the laws of either code. I am surprised that Grey is going to be in the starting line-up on Saturday.'

The Australians replied to all this with what was possibly a justified complaint that the Lions had done their best to take Larkham out of the series, the Wallabies stand-off taking three late hits, from Quinnell, Johnson and Henderson, which earned penalties. The best the Lions could offer in reply to this was another statement by Larder which said: 'We obviously realise that Stephen Larkham and George Gregan are two key players in their team – they are the guys who organise the shots – so obviously, we have got to put them under as much pressure as we can, but it was all legal. We just tried to close down their space and put them on their backsides as often as we could. The more times Stephen Larkham is on the floor, the better; the more times he is out of the game on his backside, the better.' As always, there were rights and wrongs on both sides. Larkham had indeed been a target, as he is in any Test he plays, but he had damaged his elbow trying to tackle Henderson in the First Test.

There was also a decided measure of about-face in the home media. 'The Wallabies clobber British Lions 35–14,' said the *Sydney Morning Herald*, who a week previously had condemned 'Abominable Australia'. The *Brisbane Sunday*

Mail's splash headline screeched: 'Wallabies slam wretched Lions.' Their rugby correspondent Jim Tucker (yes, real name) wrote: 'Just a week after being written off, the Wallabies produced the most stunning of form reversals. The incredible night had a pulse more like a rock concert with the decibels generated by the fans of both sides under the closed roof at Colonial stadium. The world champions ran out into the cauldron of fans with a huge point to prove, not just to themselves but their fans and acidic sections of the British media.'

The day after the Melbourne Test the acidic sections of the British media were back in the Manly Pacific, along with players, management and camp followers. The odd thing was that while the Lions players seemed to be visibly shrinking the number of journalists were multiplying by the minute, the importance of the tour denouement signalled by the arrival of a large gang of the heavies, the big-name columnists. There were even more Octagon people, too, most of whose job definitions seemed even more vague than before. In an unguarded moment one of them admitted that he had absolutely nothing to do except occasionally help lift Lions gear into the coach for training. When one of them was entrusted to drive a couple of the kickers back to the hotel he promptly ran out of petrol.

This same camp helper's passing resemblance to Matt Perry made him a popular target for myopic autograph hunters and to his credit he always put them right, before adding: 'I'm actually a member of the management.' The rest of the time was spent walking around the hotel lobby in Lions uniform swollen with self-importance. The Octagon gang sneered at the journalists and we sneered right back, but they did have a decided justification for their superiority complex and the thought of them having unlimited access to the dressing room and touchline while we sweated in the stand was galling in the extreme. At the end of the final whistle in Sydney some of them looked dangerously close to joining in the Lions' lap of honour.

Something was subtly different about Manly, too. For a start we had all been placed in sea-facing rooms, but there wasn't a lot to see: just rain coming down in sheets. Even the weather had turned against the Lions. We arrived on the Sunday night just in time to cheer on Goran Ivanisevic in the Wimbledon final against Pat Rafter, or 'the heroic Pat Rafter, the archetypal Australian sportsman' as the home press liked to put it. Rafter was that Australian rarity, a gallant loser, and he seemed a great guy, but if Slobodan Milosevic had been on the opposite side of the net we would have given three hearty cheers for him. Most of us had always considered Ivanisevic one of the lunatic brats sport could well do without, but he was definitely one of ours that night. Our support, however, didn't go down too well with one of the Lions baggage handlers, an Australian. 'What do you want to support that wog for?' was one of his milder interventions. One of the photographers won the race to take him outside and give him a good hiding. The tour seemed to be deteriorating in every way possible.

Wilkinson made an astonishing recovery when we had all virtually written him off and was duly named in the team for the final Test, testimony to the healing powers of water as he had done most of his rehabilitation in the swimming pool. Corry was in in place of Hill while Dawson finally got his starting spot at scrum-half with Healey taking over the right wing spot from Dafydd James. It meant Dawson had yet another crack at redemption and Healey would be meeting his old mate Justin Harrison, who had taken David Giffin's place at lock in the Wallaby side. What a story; we descended on both of them. This had not been on the management agenda and they were apoplectic. Their revenge was cunningly conceived: in future the media would no longer be allowed on the Lions floor and future press conferences would take place at Manly Rugby Union Club, a debilitating 400-yard walk away. A sign went up at the foot of the first-floor steps: only Lions allowed up here, or words to that effect. That was telling us.

The first interview in our new home turned out to be with Dawson, presumably as a sop and to prevent open mutiny among the discontented journos, and we duly filed into a room smelling of stale beer, cigarettes and wet carpet. Dawson was placed on a bar stool in front of a Formica-topped table, looking for all the world like something out of Dotheboys Hall, where he proceeded to produce what even the most uncharitable had to admit was a pretty polished performance. He looked cheeky, but controlled and made all the right noises about pulling together for the team. He revealed a remarkable upswing in morale, mainly due to a night out in Sydney where all the squad had got legless together. But there again with Howley out and a Lions Test starting spot his, most of his previous complaints were no longer valid. When someone plucked up the courage to ask if he had any regrets about his newspaper comments, however, Dawson went into best Ministry of Defence 'no comment' mode, replying: 'This is not the time or place to be talking about that. I don't think it's apt.' Behind him Broun nodded with a mixture of relief and approval. 'I closed that chapter as soon as I possibly could. I know I was wrong to write that piece at the time. Any talking to be done on that issue should be done at the end of the tour. There is no difficulty in the relationships between myself and the management. I have shown that by my performance against the Brumbies last week and my reaction to our win. The management have shown it by picking me for the final Test. It is a fantastic honour to be chosen. The squad has its own little world. The opinions and views being expressed outside the squad are neither here nor there. This is about us and we are very well aware of what is at stake.' You could say he had changed his tune.

There was an end-of-season, end-of-tour feeling about Manly as the days passed ever so slowly towards that final Test. The bars were still packed with Lions fans, but the sidewalks were empty after dusk and the town began to take on all the appealing aspects of Southport in

137

mid-winter. The Lions players outside the Test team started to come out at night, hanging round in bars and resignedly waiting to go home. A few said they couldn't wait.

On the Friday we were back in the Manly Arms to hear Lenihan and Henry make the team announcement. This time three Formica-topped tables had been pushed together and were going bow-legged under the weight of microphones, tape recorders and Henry's water. It all seemed a bit shabby, even more so when the afternoon was adroitly hijacked by the former New Zealand No 8 Murray Mexted, dressed all in black, plugging some coaching courses run by himself and the great Sean Fitzpatrick. He had brought videos and business cards and we dutifully sat and listened to his spiel because, well, he was Murray Mexted and was only trying to earn a crust like the rest of us. But was this, as Dawson would have put it, the right time and place? Only the wildest optimist would believe that on the eve of a deciding Lions Test he would get a free plug for International Rugby Academy New Zealand Limited.

Henry, in the short time we had him at the press conference, looked relaxed and confident and even informed us he had slept with his wife the previous night and it was 'very pleasant'. His good mood could not last, however, not with this Lions squad. On the Saturday morning someone fresh from logging off the Internet pointed out that there had been another bylined piece in a newspaper that the head coach may consider worth a look: Austin Healey had put his name to a newspaper article which made Dawson's subversive effort look like a contribution by Patience Strong. Henry pounded the hotel's front desk in frustration.

WILD COLONIAL JOY

This time the offending article was in the *Guardian* – strange how it was the quality papers and not the red-top tabloids who were producing all the contentious stuff – but this time while Austin Healey had kept criticisms of the management to a minimum he took it upon himself to lambast virtually everything Australian, with his old pal from the Brumbies, Justin Harrison, the main target. With David Giffin injured – the Australians also lost Larkham earlier in the week with a damaged elbow, Elton Flatley taking his place – Harrison had rightly been picked to partner John Eales in the Wallabies' second row and this seemed to strike a raw nerve with Healey. There was also a possibly justifiable – but totally unstructured – attack on the Australian media which read like a piece of Birkenhead graffiti. His article included such gems as: 'Spin this, you Aussies: up yours. Is that enough to get into the *Sydney Morning Sun Telegraph Herald* Load of Shite? If ever I wanted to do something, it was beat you lot. To be honestly honest – and, look, I've given you everything bar the mutiny scoop – I said it was just great to be here in the team at last. It is. But I can't help feeling for Dafydd James. He's out and I'm in. It's not as if he's done anything wrong, really. You know this hasn't been a bundle of laughs, this tour. Just imagine what it must be like if you get to the final match and find yourself dropped. Still, I think I might have been in with a shout of a place for the Second Test. But then I was injured in the ACT game. Something else I have to thank my mate Justin Harrison for. I thought it was that flanker Peter Ryan who clouted me, but, no, there it is on video, my old pal, the plod from the second row. And what do you know, he's in the team to face us. Me and the plank. Do you think one of us will have the final say? I'll say so. Did I say the weather has been crap? Just another Australian thing to get up your nose. What is it with this country? The females and children are fine, and seem to be perfectly normal human beings, but what are we going to do with this thing called the Aussie male?'

If Lenihan and the Lions management had been honest they would probably have admitted that Healey was in the high-risk category as a tourist. The incidents at the press conference after the New South Wales match and his clashes with Harrison at the ACT Brumbies game must have told them that here was an accident waiting to happen. Some journalists – challenged by Healey to arm-wrestle 'so's I can hurt you' or a round of golf and 'I'll play on my knees and still beat you' – could willingly have confirmed that point. Photographers taking pictures of the Lions in the swimming pool of the hotel in Townsville can recall Healey bombing into the deep end, just below a sign that read 'No Diving'. At Bruce Stadium he committed the not-quite-done sin of mocking the Brumbies players after scoring his interception try; looking back over his shoulder at them in his best cheeky way and gesturing as he ran in under the posts. Even his running style – all stuck-out bum and twinkling legs – had a taunting quality about it. And as one Australian journalist cleverly put it: 'Austin Healey? Good little engine, but a soft top.'

Healey was also originally from Merseyside where the feeling that fate had dealt you an unfair succession of losing cards was a way of life. He was also under medium height, another crucial paranoiac element. Like a succession of Liverpudlian comedians (Jimmy Tarbuck, Tom O'Connor etc), footballers (Joey Jones, Jimmy Case), politicians (Derek Hatton) and the *Big Brother* winner, Healey also plainly believed that his role in life was to be the eternal cheeky chappie. He was here to entertain us.

Unlike Dawson's remarks, Healey's comments were aimed not at the Lions management but Australia and Australians as a whole and lacked his England team-mate's perception and intelligence. He told friends in private that he hated Australians, a feeling dating back apparently to Bob Dwyer's tenure as Leicester coach when the two had never got on. Apologists for Healey pointed out that not only was he a rugby player of rare instinct but also that he had been to rough, tough St Anselm's College in Birkenhead, where the pupils often suffered ritualistic thrashings with a thick leather strap and the occasional outright assault with a fist, a chair leg or a blackboard duster. He was also an asthmatic with all the obstacles that complaint provides for a professional sportsman. James Robson, the Lions doctor, kept a Ventolin spray among the lotions and bandages in his medical bag on the touchline specifically for Healey and the player would often need a puff mid-game.

The *Guardian* seemed an unlikely medium for what was basically a racist rant and the comments were ghosted not by the newspaper's chief rugby writer, Robert Kitson, but the former Welsh captain Eddie Butler of the *Observer*, Kitson probably quite rightly deciding he would distance himself from such salacious stuff. Butler had no such qualms and waded in gratefully.

Healey had set sail from Britain with almost naive enthusiasm and bright-eyed optimism. As a tourist in 1997 he had plainly bought into the Lions thing, writing early after arriving in Australia: 'Because we are going to break down the best defence in the world – the Wallabies – then we're going to have to test them with something different. As the best analysers of the game, the Australians will have an idea of what they're up against. If we can't offer anything new, it'll be a story of two fantastic defences slugging it out. It'll be a series of massive collisions. I know the Lions defence will be stronger than ever. Phil Larder has been working already on a few adjustments. We have to do more than slug it out. I think everybody realises that and is ready to take on board whatever the plan is going to be. Everybody is up for it. It's what makes the challenge

141

so absorbing. But to be honest, that is what the Lions is all about. Whether you are a Celt or an Englishman, you are fighting for the same cause. It will be the same on Friday. when the first ball is kicked in anger. It will be all hands to the pump, all for one and one for all.'

So far so good, but by the time the Third Test arrived Butler/Healey decided this was a bit tame and it was time to do some winding-up. What they probably didn't appreciate is that while Australians are the world's best at handing out insults, they are not very good at taking them and it is usually considered bad form Down Under to bad-mouth someone who is not 'a mate'. His comments were seen as an abuse of their famous hospitality. The tone of Healey's piece was also decidedly non-British and quite out of character for a Lion, supposedly the noble bearer of a proud tradition. Butler – also a former Lion – later sprang gamely to Healey's defence, taking almost complete responsibility and destroying forever the fantasies of the small minority of the British newspaper-reading public who actually still believed the players wrote their columns themselves. Use of the word 'ape' to describe Harrison, said Butler, was purely his idea; 'plank' and 'plod' came from earlier discussions with Healey. The source of the rant about the Australian weather, male population and Australian journalists was not revealed. Butler's defence could not stop world opinion descending on poor, bewildered Healey like a ton of bricks. Lenihan confirmed that the Rugby Football Union were considering charging him with bringing the game into disrepute, warning: 'We are aware of the emotional difficulties these guys are under in these circumstances but that is no excuse to make derogatory comments about individuals or countries.'

Leicester chief executive Peter Wheeler, effectively Healey's employer, was also unimpressed, saying: 'Dean Richards (the Leicester coach) and I have spoken about it. We clearly need to have a look at exactly what has been said. If we believe it damages the club's name or the game of rugby, we will take action against him. Wheeler spoke for almost everyone when he added: 'There is no way the players should be writing columns in the press during Lions tours.'

The reaction in the Australian press was predictable: universal outrage that someone should be so disrespectful to their great country and great rugby players. There was talk about revoking his visa, one former player demanded that Healey should be placed in the NTA (never tour again) category. Nick Farr-Jones, the Wallabies captain of 1989, could finally, after 12 years of waiting, see ultimate revenge looming and really put the boot in: 'If management cannot keep a lid on the public spill of vitriol from their own camp on tour what chance have they of doing so when some of these clowns return to their own little support bases? But I suspect the spillage will come only from those who have reason to be uncertain about their playing futures, not those tried and tested, who return with honour.'

Healey was totally unfazed by this and promised more of the same in his forthcoming autobiography. The fact that he had given all his best stuff to the *Guardian* certainly didn't put his publisher off and he promised: 'Austin knows he won't be involved in the next Lions tour so he intends to say exactly what he thinks about what went on in Australia, especially as Clive Woodward, for whom he has great respect, was not part of the management team. He told me before the tour that he hated Australians. That goes back to when Bob Dwyer was coach at Leicester. Their relationship was so bad that Austin considered giving up rugby.' Maybe Dwyer wasn't as bad as we thought.

All sorts of unlikely folk queued up to clip Healey behind the ear, including the former England manager Dick Best, who said Healey was in danger of becoming rugby's clown – even Healey knew that – before adding the ultimate put-down: 'He is becoming England's version of David Campese, who has always had a loose wire between his brain and his mouth.'

Henry's opinion was predictable: 'I am amazed that a Lions player would give the opposition the ammunition they needed to prepare for the Test. I am amazed, too, that anyone would write that stuff on the morning of the game. It was effectively a team talk for the Australians. Healey's view was probably that he would knock them off their equilibrium, that they would be thinking of other things and so lose their focus. Instead, it was ideal ammunition for them.'

The most balanced comment came from the injured Wallaby Giffin who said – in a ghosted newspaper column: 'This is not an individual sport so when you make comments like Healey did you not only hurt yourself, you hurt your entire team. It didn't give us an extra incentive to do well. This was a massive game in its own right and there's got to be something wrong with you if you need further incentive to win that sort of match. I suppose it might have made Justin Harrison more determined but he was very focused in the game and played really well – as we expected him to.'

Harrison had been well enough motivated before Healey's intervention according to Joe Roff, who claimed that the lock had been wound up by another member of the Lions party after the Brumbies match who when asked what he thought of Harrison replied: 'He's a soft lardarse.'

Harrison was an interesting character who had only taken up rugby after leaving school. He was also a graduate of Lismore University – so hardly a 'plank' – and already something of a folk hero among his countrymen, not only for taking the Lions line-out apart whenever he had played them, but also for getting arrested for disorderly behaviour in Dunedin after a Brumbies Super 12 match. Apparently Harrison had attempted to drive a car while under the influence. He was a bit of a larrikin and as the decisive Third Test approached we were all positively slavering at the mouth at the prospect of Healey's reunion with his chum in front of 80,000 baying fans in Stadium Australia. It was not to be.

On the morning of the Test I was getting into the lift in the Manly Pacific when the former Scotland captain Andy Nicol stepped out. He looked unusually serious and preoccupied and it was only after the lift doors closed that it struck me: Nicol, not even selected for Lenihan's first sixty-seven-strong party back in February, was wearing full Lions training togs. A lot of people in the party, as we have seen, chose to dress themselves up as Lions, but on Nicol it did seem more significant. It emerged then that Healey, despite the work of a local chiropractor, had failed to recover from back spasms and had been ruled out the evening before. As well as leaving Healey with large dollops of egg all over his face, this put the Lions in something of a dilemma. Howley was irreversibly out with cracked ribs and with Healey *hors de combat*, too, there was no cover for Dawson, it always being assumed that Healey would be subbed on the wing and take over at scrum-half if anything happened to the first-choice No 9.

It was also, even in these days of supersonic air travel, far too late to send for a replacement. Then someone remembered; they had spotted TWO international scrum-halfs wandering round Manly, one being Nicol, the other Rupert Moon, the former Welsh No 9. Moon, who was there with friends and obviously in holiday mode, was considered more of a risk than the more serious-minded Nicol who in his capacity as a tour guide, should also be in possession of all his mental and physical faculties. In other words, in a hastily arranged training session he could be trusted not to breathe beer fumes over his new team-mates. Thus it was that Scotland's thirty-year-old deposed captain, who hadn't even seen a rugby ball since the beginning of May, found himself on the bench in the deciding Test of a Lions series. Nicol recalled later: 'The Lions manager Donal Lenihan got me just as I was about to leave the hotel to climb the Sydney Harbour Bridge and he said that was a good sign because you have to be sober to do that – and you do, you get breathalysed before you go up. He told me that they would

145

wait for results from tests on Austin Healey and if the news was bad, would call me into the squad in the morning. So, there was me, at 11p.m. on the Friday night, when the Lions squad are wrapped up in bed with their cocoa, standing on top of Sydney Harbour Bridge. I could see loads of Lions fans down below, at The Rocks restaurants and bars, and could hear them signing *Flower of Scotland, Bread of Heaven* and *Cockles and Mussels* and it was just unbelievable.' It was unbelievable for a lot of other people, too, and to many seemed symptomatic of the decay that had eaten into the 2001 Lions since defeat in Melbourne. It was hardly the fault of Nicol, but even Henry was astonished that after taking out the largest number of players for the shortest itinerary in the team's history they now had to recruit a tour guide off a Sydney beach for the deciding Test. 'It seemed extraordinary to face a search for a replacement the night before a crucial Test when we started with thirty-seven, the largest tour party ever,' said the coach.

Fortunately, Nicol had been keeping himself fit in Australia by running every day but it was still a big ask. On the Saturday morning he threw maybe three passes to Jonny Wilkinson and stood and watched half a dozen line-outs. The Australians knew more of the coded calls than him. Fortunately, he was never called on in the match. The Australians, meanwhile, had discovered another reason to win on the Saturday: this time they were doing it for Rod. Macqueen had announced after the Melbourne Test that he would step down at the end of the series rather than continue, as planned, into the Tri Nations. A win in Stadium Australia would give him a record of thirty-nine Test wins, eight losses and a draw and make him the most successful coach in rugby history and the Australian media machine sprang into action, wheeling out a long line of players to swear that beating the Lions would prove a suitable send-off.

'You can't go on forever, you've got to make a decision at some stage and I'd rather make that decision sooner than later,' said Macqueen. 'Your effectiveness wears off after a while. I've been there four years and it's time to go. I'm sure in a few weeks time I'll start to get the cravings but certainly I'm very comfortable with the decision.' Being comfortable and in control is his hallmark. Defeat is something that has never sat well.

Macqueen's decision also meant that the international rugby world had to brace itself for Eddie Jones a little earlier than anticipated although Macqueen did reveal: 'He's been with us since day one, he's been part of the programme that we've put together and mimicked that with Australia A. It's an easy transition. That's made the decision a lot easier for me, the fact that I know there's a good person there.'

Driving from Manly into Sydney on the evening of the Second Test there was more proof that God is an Australian as, passing Darling Harbour, the sky lit up into a spectacular sunset. It was a golden sunset, notable for an absence of red. For the first time, too, the Wallaby fans had answered the ARU gathering call and the Lions support were out-numbered. Down below the press box a small army of gold-shirted, middle-aged Australians troughed away in their corporate boxes complete with individual TV sets and served by one harassed waitress bearing sandwiches, sausage rolls and plastic beer glasses. As at Sydney Football Stadium and a lot of other venues, there was a feeling that this was a rugby-illiterate nation, that they would turn up to support anything in green and gold playing anything British and that the on-field action seemed an excuse for something else.

There also seemed a strangely subdued atmosphere in the ground, despite the magnificence of the Olympic Stadium. This was not helped by ranks of empty seating where the north terracing was being rebuilt and where in an inane gesture the ARU – following the example of Arsenal and their famous cardboard frieze of fans – had encased the seats in yellow, plastic bags in an effort to convince everyone that these were really Australian supporters in disguise. There was no Pat Rafter this time, either; he had gone and lost so this time it was the Australian cricketers shouting 'Go Wallabies Go' on the big screen.

The match, as they say, went right to the wire and was magnificent as a sporting spectacle. But the rugby was of pretty poor quality with a stream of penalties and aimless kicking away of possession dominating the first forty minutes. The Lions were also plainly attempting to draw on something that they no longer possessed and perhaps the most revealing statistic of the whole series was the fact that they failed to score a single point in the last quarter of each Test match. In the same period the Wallabies scored thirty, including three tries. That the Lions ultimately failed by just six points was a miracle in itself.

Much of the credit for this must go to the warrior king who led them, for if any one man has transfixed a sporting event by sheer personality it was Johnson. His insistence later that 'the eighty minutes between the kick-off and the final whistle is ours and we messed it up; you can only blame the players' was a brave thing to say, but didn't find much assent. That they lost could have been put down to their loss of control at crucial times, a wobbly line-out and the ability of the Australians – George Smith in particular – to win possession on the ground, but really they were dipping into an empty well. You couldn't blame the players for that.

Harrison, with or without the inspiration provided by Healey, had a superb, snarling match at the heart of the Wallabies pack and struck a crucial psychological blow within a minute, winning the first Lions ball at the first line-out. When Finegan charged, the Lions were caught offside at the ruck and Burke opened the scoring with a penalty. Wilkinson – who only four days earlier had been on crutches – emphatically proved his fitness with a tackle on Larkham's replacement Elton Flatley that left the Australian needing lengthy attention, and the English stand-off lev-elled the scores from in front of the posts when Michael

Foley took Henderson out with a blatant bodycheck. Burke kicked his second penalty when Quinnell tried to run the ball out of his own 22, was nailed by Andrew Walker and, with Smith scrabbling for the ball the Welshman failed to release. Quinnell repeated the offence five minutes later and Burke punished the Lions again. Robinson was soon over in the corner, Wilkinson converting spectacularly from the touchline, and the seven points put the Lions in the lead for first time at 10–9. But there was a fragility about their play and the lead looked just as nebulous. Ominously, Wilkinson missed three straightforward penalties and the Wallabies scented blood. The Lions made another hash of a restart and George Gregan worked the short side for Walker and Roff to put Daniel Herbert over. Burke's conversion made it 16–10 and the fans below in the corporate boxes almost choked on their chicken legs.

Another penalty from Wilkinson made the score 16–13 with the last kick of the half and with only three points dividing the teams the Lions still, incredibly, had the series within their grasp. Henry pleaded in the dressing room: 'Our whole character is at stake this half. The British Lions' character is at stake, whether you've got the guts or not. The Australians don't think you have. Have you got the character?'

Well, yes and no. Quinnell, who as it transpired had trained little all week, did not reappear, Charvis taking his place, but the Lions made a sensational start to the second forty minutes with their forwards driving in an unstoppable red tide and Wilkinson dancing over for a try that he converted himself. It was 20–16 to the Lions, but then came one of those seminal moments beloved of sportswriters everywhere. Ten minutes into the half the Wallabies won a penalty near the posts. An easy three points for Burke, but Eales opted for the line-out and a few phases later hooker Foley, out in the centres, put Herbert over for his second try.

Herbert the hero turned sinner within a minute with a

tackle that almost took O'Driscoll's head off, the centre being yellow-carded and Wilkinson kicking the penalty that levelled the scores at 23–23, but the Lions could not take advantage. Australia ran down the clock expertly and, when Herbert returned, the score was still locked. The Wallabies made them pay in typical fashion when Grewcock obstructed Harrison at a line-out and Burke made the score 26–23 with another penalty. When Charvis handled on the ground with five minutes left, the full-back took his side two scores clear again.

Finally, Harrison's moment of glory. With one minute and fifty seconds to go, the Lions forced a line-out inside the Wallabies 22 and Wood took the banker option, throwing short and hard to Johnson at the front. Harrison rose at the same time and grabbed the ball. As Harrison said later: 'The boys were into me; they didn't want to contest the line-out. But I was firing back at them that I did want to contest it. I knew it was a tough time for the Lions, and a tough time for us. As their captain, I thought they would look to Johnson for inspiration, and I was pretty sure he'd call the line-out to himself. A lot of things had to go right, and they all did. I think the moons were aligned for me tonight, and I'll probably go out and buy a lottery ticket tomorrow.'

There was time for one more line-out. This time the Lions threw deeper and mounted a series of attacks reminiscent of the Brumbies game. As the final hooter sounded the Lions had, finally, established an overlap about 15 metres out from the Wallaby try line, but the final pass went behind Balshaw and Walker happily ran the ball into touch.

At the end Johnson and Wood, captain and deputy, embraced. Johnson made arrangements to swap jerseys with Eales and Black and the rest of the coaching staff did their best to console the players, many of them in tears. The Octagon gang spilled on to the pitch to take a bow, along with the Australian Prime Minister, John Howard, complete with his free Wallaby scarf. Quite rightly he was greeted by a storm of Australian boos as he presented the spoils to Eales.

Finally, the Lions trooped off to look for a quiet place to hide. Back in the dressing room Lenihan made a short, moving speech before emotion overcame him. The Lions players applauded; Henry's contribution was received in silence. Wood revealed later: 'At that stage I was beyond tears. Losers' changing rooms are the same the world over, lonely, desolate places with nowhere to hide. This one was all the more desolate because of the magnitude of the occasion. It was horrible.'

At the gloom-laden press conference Johnson, who looked absolutely numbed, praised the Wallabies as 'the best-drilled and the best-prepared team we have ever come up against'. He added, to what sounded suspiciously like ironic applause from the Aussie TV crews: 'They are always extremely well prepared, and get the best out of everything they have; that is why they are world champions. They were very cute in the line-out tonight, and that was an area where we lost a lot of possession. I have to say that half the Lions team were held together with sticky tape, but that is not to make excuses. The lads are very down and disappointed in the dressing room.'

Henry managed to say the right things, too: 'You wouldn't have sent out a school XV with some of those injuries. But I am so proud of what we have achieved. The Wallabies deserved to win because they were more efficient than we were when it mattered. We lost the ball at crucial times, showed poor discipline in the first half and were inconsistent with our short side defence especially on Australia's first try. But as Martin Johnson, the captain, said, our players were really only held together by sticky tape after the exhaustion of an eleven-month season and the deluge of tour injuries. Having said that, we didn't let anyone down. The players showed real guts and tenacity. As a group we felt we'd given it our best shot. But just hadn't been good enough on the day. We'll have to live with the fact that we had the prize within our grasp, but we just couldn't close our fingers around it. The one that got away.'

And with no prizes awarded for guesswork, he added: 'We had a couple of bad apples on tour with us but I'd rather not stoop to their level by saying what I think about them here. What I will say is that I'll never understand why being chosen for the Lions squad is not seen as a great honour. And I can't explain why any player would put their own importance above that of the team.' Back out on the pitch Macqueen also delivered his famous last words: 'It was a very special effort from the players. It is a nice way to go out on the basis of how they played. It was a very tight game, and I was very pleased with the composure our guys showed. It is the little things that count, and they were probably the difference between the two teams.'

With a final wave to the crowd he added: 'It's bloody good to be Australian.' As the sound of the jolly swagman camping by a billabong rang out over the stadium for the hundredth time and the resolutely defiant red hordes departed to their coaches and hotels the feeling was that over the next two days, before we climbed gratefully aboard the flight for home, it was definitely not going to be bloody good to be British or Irish.

LAST POST

Australia awoke on the morning of Sunday July 12 to the sound it enjoys most: the caterwauling of whingeing Poms, the sore losers from the Mother Country crying into their cornflakes, the battered Brits who had been shown the way home by the world champion Wallabies. Three-quarters of the nation couldn't have told Daniel Herbert from Daniel O'Donnell and probably perceived a wallaby as a sort of smaller, inferior kangaroo, but that was beside the point; the Pommies had lost. What is more, if we were to believe the Australian media, they had lost in less than gracious fashion. The Aussies proceeded to rub our noses in it. One newspaper carried a story about Justin Harrison going into the Lions dressing room in the bowels of Stadium Australia after the match to swap his shirt and being told to 'fuck off'.

'I just went in there asking who wanted to swap a jersey,' he said. 'They were obviously disappointed. There was no real reaction. Then someone yelled for me to fuck off, so I left. That was a bit disappointing. But I don't want to make anything of it.' It was later revealed that the remark came not from a Lions player but one of the small army of camp followers surrounding the tour party.

The Aussie media pounced on this, *The Australian* newspaper accusing: 'Traditions of the game were recklessly stomped as the brooding losers, showing all the petulance of schoolboy prats, refused to swap jerseys with the debutant. This was an abhorrent kick in the teeth for good sportsmanship which underlined the siege mentality that overtook their campaign.'

Healey's pre-match remarks and the fact that Harrison was named man of the match were also seized on with glee. Harrison had been paraded in the post-match press conference and wallowed in the opportunity: 'I'm pretty happy about the game I played, and he will think on his long flight home about the game he should have played.' That earned a huge collective guffaw from the Australian press pack and was a comment highlighted by the home media. In terms of handing out insults, Healey was also proved to be an also-ran.

'Motormouth Healey blasted Sydney's weather, the surf, Pat Rafter and Wallaby debutant Justin Harrison in the lead-up to the Aussies' victory. Healey withdrew from the match with back spasms. In other words, there was a question mark over his spine,' was one comment. Even Greg Growden, the man thought by the British pressmen to be the most balanced of the Australian rugby writers, had a rush of blood to the head, giving this verdict in the *Sydney Morning Herald*: 'The Lions have only themselves to blame for allowing a tour to go off the rails by letting a prat get away with writing such bile, which basically messed up six weeks of sheer, hard grind. As Wallaby officials said on Saturday morning: "Thank you, Austin. What more motivation do we need?" All tour, the Lions bled internally, with whingers like Healey and Matt Dawson repeatedly bleating in the British media about how hard life was and how horrible the management was to them. The Lions management huffed and puffed but let the players get away with this mutinous behaviour, and the moans continued unabated. All this did was show up a weakness in terms of management and leadership skills. As our esteemed colleague Evan Whitton wrote about the 1989 Lions: "The scum also rises." Twelve years on, nothing has changed.'

Eddie Jones, now the Wallabies coach officially, resurfaced to have his say: 'It obviously had an effect on the Lions. A number of the players in the Lions weren't particularly happy about it and I think it just goes back to the culture of the team.'

Nor were the British journos safe. A female commentator

decided we were guilty by association when she wrote: 'The Lions may be crucified by some of their own media, just as Tim Henman, the courageous young Englishman, was mauled when he bowed out of Wimbledon. The travelling media pack should have spent more time in the bleachers with the army of Lions supporters, if only to get lessons in decency.' It was the first time any of us could recall any UK sportsman, let alone Tim Henman, earning the description of 'a gallant young Englishman' from an Australian journalist. There was also a predictable air of triumphalism about some of the home verdicts, not all of it original. Peter Fitzsimmons, the former Wallaby forward best remembered for being stretched on the turf by a diminutive French scrum-half in a Test match punch-up, plagiarised Sir Winston Churchill to write: 'And if Australian rugby should last a thousand years, men and women will still say, this, this was its finest hour.' Not content with rewriting Churchill, Fitzsimmons then turned his attention to Sir Walter Scott: 'One hour of life, crowded to the full with glorious action, and filled with noble risks, is worth whole years of those mean observances of paltry decorum.'

The Wallabies, virtually ignored until then, were suddenly big news on TV and radio and following as it did Pat Rafter's Wimbledon, Stuart O'Grady's yellow jersey in the Tour de France and the men in baggy green caps putting Mike Atherton and Co to the sword at Lord's, Sydney was a difficult place to be on the morning after the night before. Even the Manly locals, traditionally steeped in rugby league, found it difficult to keep condescending smiles off their faces. Hasham, the friendly manager in the Spice of Manly diner next to the hotel – popular with the travelling media because of his generosity with blank receipts and the fact that you could bill food and drink to rooms – tried hard not to be condescending. 'I'm just so glad that it turned out be such a thrilling series,' he commented, trying hard not to laugh.

155

Around the Manly Pacific I could discern another noise – the unmistakable one of large knives being sharpened. As Brendan Fanning had correctly predicted a week into the tour the travelling journalists were forming an orderly queue to stick the boot in. Macqueen had not been far off the mark when he said after the Test: 'Graham and the rest will probably cop some bad press over this.' The targets were random and the damnation was spread widely. Those who abhorred the idea of a foreigner coaching the Lions blamed Henry and what they perceived as his abandonment of the traditions of the team, a disrespect implicit in his treatment of the midweek team. Others saw the Larder and Robinson training regimes as far too enervating at the end of an eleven-month season. The injuries that ended the tour for almost a third of the party were a natural consequence of this. There were mistakes in the original selection and the teams picked during the tour, most notably the omission of Martin Corry from the Second Test, while the decision not to send for another scrum-half following Rob Howley's injury in Melbourne was cited as another factor. Austin Healey was being blamed not only for the defeat in Stadium Australia but for everything ranging from foot and mouth disease to Third World debt, with Matt Dawson as a willing fellow conspirator. There was even a claim that a cutting of Healey's final offending article had been pinned to the home dressing room by Rod Macqueen as extra motivation – a major coup for the *Guardian* distribution department as the piece had only appeared in England the previous morning.

But Healey's and Dawson's were not the only dissenting voices. Colin Charvis, Neil Back, Dan Luger, Jeremy Davidson, Ben Cohen and Malcolm O'Kelly also expressed their disappointment in print at the lack of opportunities for the fringe players. Cohen, who to put it mildly had a bad year, losing his father, being burgled and receiving death threats from an fan followed by a mediocre Lions tour, said: 'I am not bitter towards the management. They had to pick what they considered the best side. But the communication was not the best.'

Jeremy Davidson, the unlikely star of the Springboks series in 1997, said in a newspaper interview of the non-Test locks – himself, Scott Murray and O'Kelly – 'The management think we're three Muppets.' O'Kelly, too, reported in the *Irish Independent* that members of the midweek 'dirt-trackers' side felt they had been overlooked from the start. 'We were inspired by the thought that there were no preconceived ideas of the Test team,' O'Kelly wrote. 'Now, one can't help feeling the Test team had been pencilled in from the start.' Even David Young, Henry's Welsh captain and a man not noted for issuing establishment views in public, was moved to remark: 'Graham has to recognise that players deserve explanations about how they were treated.'

The southern hemisphere refereeing, the orchestrated home media campaign, the poor relations with the travelling press, the carrying of injured passengers, junket-hungry administrators who had plotted a wearying season and even the nominated match balls – too light for Jonny Wilkinson's liking – also received honourable mentions as the reasons for failure. Some commentators preferred to highlight the series' so-called turning points, those illusory moments contained in every sportswriter's book of cliches. Harrison's last-minute line-out catch at Sydney, Dafydd James' failure to send Jason Robinson in under the posts in the early minutes in Melbourne, the tackle that took Richard Hill out of the series and the Jonny Wilkinson pass intercepted by Joe Roff in Melbourne were all popular choices. Many of the post-mortems came with the benefit of hindsight and in some cases the qualifications of the sources were somewhat dubious. Even the soccer writer of the *Daily Star* was moved to an opinion – from a safe distance ten thousand miles away in London: others should have known better.

The England manager Clive Woodward, the man not

considered for the Lions coaching job – although the actual England coach Andy Robinson played a leading role – weighed in with some curious contributions. Woodward, who had hopped over to Australia to act as a pundit for Sky straight after England's tour of Canada, hovered over the series like Banquo's ghost; most of his comments on the Lions and Henry demonstrated a mastery of the art of praising with faint damnation. Woodward took care not to criticise directly, but the implications were obvious when he claimed the Wallabies 'were there to be taken'.

'I am totally supportive of Graham,' he added. 'But just from what the players are saying, it is clear there have been mistakes.'

In another article he aimed a broadside at Henry for his commercial activities on the side on tour, saying; 'The highest standards have not been put forward by the Lions management from the start. It is totally wrong for Graham Henry to be writing a book. If Matt (Dawson) or Austin (Healey) had done this in the England set-up, they could only expect one result. However, if you do not set high standards at the top in this area, how can you expect the players to follow?' Woodward did, however, telephone Henry after the First Test win in Brisbane to offer his congratulations, an act that apparently astonished the Lions coach.

Woodward's contributions did not end there. On the Sunday after the Third Test he sent an e-mail to most of the leading rugby agents repeating his insistence that he would have thrown Healey and Dawson out of the England team if they had broken ranks under his command and that Henry had hardly set a good example with his off-field commitments. Woodward was amazed when the message was leaked to the national press.

Everyone, seemingly, had a solution. There were calls for players' newspaper columns to be banned – with even columnist and future author Henry arguing that a ban will be a result of this tour. 'Two years ago, players weren't writing in newspapers. I guess it's a modern trend, and they find it difficult to handle. When you're writing in the newspapers now, you want to have something to say.' The former Lions coach Ian McGeechan claimed that the tourists should have taken thirty players only and played two extra games to keep every player involved; while others echoed Henry's view that in future a tour should consist only of a couple of warm-up matches followed by the three Tests. There were calls for the squad to assemble at least a month before departure and the suspension of domestic knock-out competitions in a Lions year. There were demands for less emphasis on the commercial side; while Octagon had their own solution and demanded a full-time Lions management structure. All these things were to lead with a series victory in New Zealand in 2005.

The tour, and the injuries in particular, were to have damaging consequences back home in Britain. Dallaglio and Henderson were ruled out for six months, both with knee injuries. Scott Quinnell missed the start of the season with his club Llanelli after another knee operation. This did not go down too well with a lot of employers. Wasps, Dallaglio's club, immediately announced that they would sue the Lions for compensation, even though the injury had been suffered in what most good judges had seen as totally meaningless end-of-season Premiership play-offs.

The intransigent mood of the club owners and their insistence on commercial realism was perhaps best summed up by an interview with the Bristol chairman Malcolm Pearce in the magazine *Rugby World*. He said: 'I actually find it blooming funny with all this talk about players needing rest. If Bristol have a good cup run this season we'll play about twenty-eight matches and that's a total of thirty-seven and a half hours' rugby. Not much is it? Yes, I know they train, but so do people in all sorts of jobs. I have every sympathy with Wasps. If someone wants to use one of your employees for a bit of moonlighting – which is essentially what these tours are – and he comes back damaged, then of course you want compensation. We're not in the amateur days any more.'

Most of the post-mortems, however, failed to take into account one important factor: the make-up of the opposition. By the end of the tour it was obvious that while on paper the Lions were far stronger in the departments of talent, physical strength and flair, the Wallabies had something else, something intangible that had less to do with sporting ability and more to do with simply being Australian, something deep within the national psyche. For me, the defining moments of the tour were not on the field of play.

In Canberra, on the Wednesday following the narrow squeak against ACT Brumbies, the Lions management booked yet another hotel room to announce the side for the Second Test. Spirits were remarkably high. Henry, arrived in what appeared on the surface to be lingering festive mode. His face was as red as a Lions jersey and he smirked constantly at no one in particular in the assembled press throng while gulping down glass after glass of water. The New Zealand accent was even thicker and his hands scrabbled involuntarily and nervously at his shirt sleeves. If he had been celebrating a successful few days in time-honoured fashion then no one surely could blame him. If the strains of the tour had caused high blood pressure he had our every sympathy. With a Test victory in his pocket and a win from behind against Australia's strongest Super 12 side, it proved he was only human. His celebratory mood was infectious. Following the press conference the players named in the squad for the Second Test in Melbourne were available for interview and as Lenihan and Henry had named twenty-seven, this meant virtually all of them. This time they all turned up. The contrast between that session and the one in Manly a week previously before the First Test could not have been more marked and the Lions came as close to happy co-operation as any time on tour. They were positively falling over themselves to meet the press. Sarah Mockford, the young journalism trainee, had a benevolent Martin Johnson to herself for a ten-minute interview and half an hour later she could be seen earnestly quizzing Jonny Wilkinson in a one-on-one chat. He wasn't even yawning. Matt Dawson, the restored hero of the hour following his last-minute conversion against ACT, was besieged and took the opportunity to restate his contrition and tell us all what it meant to be a Lion. There were some predictable sound bytes about there being a long way to go and you should never underestimate the Wallabies, particularly from an unusually serious Keith Wood, but the scent of a series victory was in the air.

Afterwards, in a mood best described as passive euphoria I decided to break the habit of a lifetime to go sightseeing and, along with Nick Cain of the *Sunday Times*, walked the mile and a half from the centre of Canberra up Anzac Parade to the foot of Mount Ainslie where the Australian War Memorial is sited. Anzac Parade is a wide avenue stretching from the city's lake shore and is lined not only by a thousand trees but also at intervals of a hundred metres or so monuments to the Australian dead of every field of conflict in the country's history, including Korea and Vietnam. There were soaring memorials to the Royal Australian Air Force, the Rats of Tobruk and the Australian Service Nurses and even an elaborate circular paved area and wall to remember Kemal Ataturk, the man who commanded the Turkish forces who fought and slaughtered the Anzacs at Gallipoli.

The Memorial itself, at the eastern end of the avenue, is built of sandstone and has an almost Byzantine profile at stark odds with the rest of purpose-built Canberra. There are lawns and eucalyptus and evidence on the ground of the occasional nocturnal visit of kangaroos, or maybe wallabies. The Memorial had recently been revitalised by a 20-million-dollar development programme – the cash raised by public subscription – and the result is startling.

161

Wide steps lead into the commemorative courtyard where the Tomb of the Unknown Australian Soldier overlooks a placid pool. Every Australian serviceman and woman killed in war, 102,000 in all, is remembered there by name. Inside there are extensive exhibitions and research facilities and around twenty galleries depicting Australians at war, along with works of art. The memorial and its exhibits close every day at 5p.m. and on the day we were there we were invited, by one of the many unpaid, voluntary guides, to gather at the opposite end of the pool to the Unknown Soldier as the *Last Post* sounded and the doors of the tomb closed slowly. It was a remarkably moving experience made even more extraordinary by the sight of some forty Australian primary schoolchildren standing silently to attention, facing the tomb, with eyes closed. All this was totally spontaneous; next to me a tear trickled down the cheek of a braided-hair blonde girl no more than five years old. I tried to imagine this happening in Manchester, Liverpool or London and couldn't.

Walking back through the Canberra suburbs towards the city centre and our hotel, I pondered again the unfathomable contradictions of Australia, a nation that could elect a monster like Labour Prime Minister Bob Hawke (famous for calling an old age pensioner 'a silly old bugger' on camera) to power and yet whose children weep over the dead of a war that pre-dated their grandparents. A country that constitutes six independent state governments and which until 1991 had differing legal procedures, electrical power and road systems – even different definitions on the packaging of margarine – and yet which could still combine wholeheartedly to support an entity representing that nation, be they called Wallabies, Kangaroos, Pat Rafter or the Aussie Cricket XI. A country where the service personnel, be it a taxi driver, waitress or barman, considers a tip demeaning and yet who plaster advertising on virtually anything that moves. A people proud of their independence of thought but who exist in what amounts to a nanny state

162

with its continual 'Do Nots' plastered on the consciousness. A nation that still weeps and wails over bodyline and yet which believes that Trevor Chappell's underarm ball against New Zealand in 1981 was a legitimate tactic and who can still carp bitterly about the perceived violence visited on the Wallabies during the Lions tour of 1989 and yet dismiss as whingeing Poms the English who recall the far more violent Battle of Ballymore in 1975. In Sydney Jason Robinson had been stopped in the street by an Australian who asked what the NTL logo on his shirt meant and, before Robinson could explain, the man interrupted to say: 'I thought it meant "No Talent, Lads."' Yet the same country could produce people happy to invite tourists, total strangers, back to their homes.

So many anomalies. But it was the sight of the little girl at the Tomb of the Unknown Soldier that began to raise serious doubts about the chances of Australia losing on their home soil: even at that age there was pride in the country's short history and heritage. How clever of Rod Macqueen, then, before one Test match, to give a speech that invoked the spirit of an Aussie soldier from the First World War and even the bauble that the Lions and the Wallabies were fighting over, the Tom Richards Trophy, took its name from a First Word War veteran.

And then there was Lyndon (named after the Hanoi bomber LBJ), a cheerful redneck labourer, clad in traditional togs of shorts and bush boots, who I met in a Manly bar three days before the final Test. Like many Australians Lyndon was quite willing to engage a total stranger in intimate conversation, on his terms. By then I had learned the dos and donts. I accepted, for example, that using first names within seconds of meeting an Australian signals some mystical equality and that one should never react adversely to bad language or insults. Obsessed almost exclusively by the pursuit of girls and a love of drinking, he was, on the surface at least, the archetypal Aussie okker, loud, brash and not too bright. He brought back

163

the memory of Donald Horne's definition of the Aussie male who spent their lives 'standing around bars asserting their masculinity with such intensity that you half-expect them to unzip their flies'. Within an hour we were 'mates' for life, the mateship announced by his non-stop supply of insults and total delight when I responded in kind. I was a 'fucking Pommie bastard'; he was a convict clod, the usual sort of thing. He shared the pathological fear and hatred of 'poofters' of so many of his countrymen and his hero was the former PM Hawke, who had announced his marital infidelity in public and 'showed he was one of us'. But Lyndon also came close to crying on my shoulder when describing the recent death of his grandfather, who had fought the Japanese in Burma. We made drunken plans – with certain reservations on my part – to meet later that week to 'drink Manly dry and shag some local hot drops'. He could not, however, make it the next night. He had a regular engagement every Wednesday to drive some of his grandfather's friends – all in their eighties – down to the Manly Returned Servicemen's League for a game of bridge. As we parted he must have read my mind and said quietly, and almost sympathetically: 'Mate, the Poms will never beat the Aussies in a million years.'

On our penultimate day in Australia, players, management and the travelling Press corps began to work on the massive collective hangover that was not quite metaphorical in a lot of cases. Some of the players had failed to reappear from a night out in Sydney on Saturday night while the journalists who in some cases had worked until four in the morning emerged blinking and gasping into a bright Manly afternoon. Henry gave his final press conference as a Lions coach where he was offered the opportunity to bask in hindsight but simply insisted he would never change a thing, except perhaps scrap the midweek fixtures and concentrate on the Tests.

'From a purely rugby point of view, things do need to

change if we are to improve tours in the future,' said Henry, who appeared relaxed and almost relieved. 'The management have talked about future tours, and you're probably talking about Saturday games only and with a smaller squad. The Tuesday fixtures were very difficult because it was difficult to prepare the teams for those matches, that's our gut feeling. I just don't think it was the right thing for the players involved. The coaching staff felt for the Tuesday group of players because we just couldn't do the right preparation. The only time we had the twenty-two players together was the Monday before the Tuesday game, and these guys are used to building for a game from the Sunday through to the Saturday. We just felt it wasn't fair on them, and it was inadequate preparation, and you don't want to have that situation with quality players. Maybe it would be better to have a reduced number of players, say twenty-eight, and have a lead-in of three games, concentrating on one game a week and building to three Test matches.'

It was a reasoned argument, but those who had accused him of having little regard for the history and tradition of the red jersey nodded knowingly. The consensus of opinion, however, was that Henry would be involved in the story of the British Lions again – when he took over as New Zealand coach in time to meet the 2005 tourists on his home patch. That should be an interesting reunion.

Austin Healey, with his wife Louise, disappeared for a brief holiday in Hawaii, along with Martin Johnson and his wife Kay, unaware that within days Healey would be charged with bringing the game into disrepute and Johnson would sit, with Henry and Donal Lenihan, on an official enquiry in early September into the Case of the Leicester Lip. Behind them, the rest of the tour party shrugged off the yoke of rugby professionalism and set about drinking themselves insensible, commandeering a bar on the seafront where customers and passers-by were assailed by tuneless choruses of *Delilah* that echoed across the Pacific. Phil Vickery turned into doorman for the day, ejecting punter after punter into the street as Rob Henderson demanded: 'Let's head back into Sydney.' Back in the hotel Iain Balshaw, still with the look of bemusement he had worn on his face from the first day at Tylney Hall, sat drinking quietly with some friends from Blackburn and Phil Greening reappeared with a stunning girl in tow. At around 6p.m. as darkness fell, Ronan O'Gara was spotted engaged in his second fight of the tour. The man in the opposite corner was his Ireland team-mate Brian O'Driscoll and like the encounter with Duncan McRae at Sydney Football Stadium it should have been no contest. O'Driscoll was a schoolboy boxing champion back home in Dublin, but he was quite spectacularly drunk and O'Gara, by dint of the fact that his countryman was unable to rise from the pavement, won by technical knockout. Keith Wood, with his fiancee Nicola watching apprehensively, kissed every team-mate he could find and from then on the night disintegrated into the sort of drunken rowdyism we once used to happily associate with rugby union. At 4a.m. on the last day in Australia for the tourists, any insomniac passers-by on Manly seafront could have caught sight of Dorian West snoring peacefully on a bench, within yards of where Wood and Nicola sat arm-in-arm gazing dreamily out over a spectacular, moonlit Pacific. In the seven weeks since I had seen him in the swimming pool at Tylney Hall, Wood had played six games for the Lions, made over one hundred tackles, flogged his way through around eighty training sessions and had been hammered to the ground, punched, stood on, raked and gouged. He had put his body on the line for a mystique contained within a red jersey, just as his late father Gordon had done forty-two years previously. If anyone had bought into that priceless badge it was Wood.

It had turned out to be a losing cause. At twenty-nine, it was probably his last Lions tour, as it undoubtedly was for Johnson, Howley, Back, Charvis, Dawson, Grewcock,

Henderson, Jenkins, Leonard, Young, Quinnell . . . and Healey. But at least for one man in Manly that morning it looked as though there was life after the Lions.

In the hotel lobby next day, as we dragged hastily packed suitcases down to reception, there wasn't a player, coach, member of the management, or punter to be seen. Not even an Octagon employee. The 2001 British and Irish Lions were no more.

Appendix One

CAST AND CREW

THE MANAGEMENT

Manager: Donal Lenihan
Head Coach: Graham Henry
Assistant Coach: Andy Robinson
Defensive Coach: Phil Larder
Conditioning Coach: Steve Black
Doctor: James Robson
Video Analyst: Alun Carter
Physiotherapist: Mark Davis
Masseur: Richard Wegrzyk
Media Liaison: Alex Broun
Baggage Manager: Pat O'Keefe
Admin Assistant: Joan Moore

THE PLAYERS

NEIL BACK (Leicester and England):
Age 32. Played 5, tries 3, total 15 points.

Like one of his famous England predecessors, one Andy
Robinson, Back had spent a large part of his career trying to
prove that small is beautiful on the rugby field, that speed
to the breakdown and work rate could compensate for lack
of physical presence. Back had managed this so successfully
that he had earned forty-one international caps and two
Lions tours. But there was strong evidence in Australia
that at this level at any rate, Back's career was running
out of steam. Injured and not considered for the First Test,
the England openside flanker was thrown in to counter the
ball-snaffling skills of George Smith in the final two Tests.
Smith, however, was too fast, too strong and possibly too
young.

IAIN BALSHAW (Bath and England):
Age 22. Played 8 (3 as substitute), tries 2, total 10.

If anything summed up the vagaries of touring it was the perplexed face of the young Englishman as he stumbled around Australia from one nightmare to another. Touted as the Lions great attacking hope based on a startling Six Nations season with England where he had brought a new potency to attacking full-back play, Balshaw started off badly in Perth and went downhill from there, his confidence not helped by the inability of the management to drag him out of the doldrums. The one consolation is that there will be another chance, possibly in New Zealand in 2005. Whether he will be prepared to expose himself to this sort of experience again is a different debate.

GORDON BULLOCH (Glasgow and Scotland):
Age 26. Played 4 (3 as sub).

Bulloch had showed some fortitude and strength of charac-ter by fighting back from a shoulder injury in 2000 to win back his Scotland hooking place and, although disappointed to miss the first flight out with the Lions, was eventually called in as cover for Robin McBryde when the Welshman went down with injury. A place on the bench for the Second Test was his reward, but he was swiftly discarded when the England hooker Dorian West arrived. This may have been, as Bulloch later implied, an Anglo-Saxon plot to keep him on the sidelines or simply the fact that West was up to speed with England (Lions) defensive drills and thus better qualified.

MIKE CATT (Bath and England):
Age 29. Played 1.

Should he have stayed or should he have gone? A key man

in Henry's plans for his passing ability and auxiliary kicker to Wilkinson (and even reserve stand-off), Catt in the end simply became one of the small army of walking wounded who were hanging around the tour for what seemed like weeks in the hope that the sun and salt sea of Australia would provide a rehabilitating miracle for their injuries. Catt eventually passed a fitness test and played a half and a bit of the Australia A game before breaking down. Seemed to be enjoying himself before he went home, though.

COLIN CHARVIS (Swansea and Wales):
Age 28. Played 6 (4 as sub), tries 3, total 15.

The Wales flanker probably had a point when he claimed, constantly, that the Test team had been set in stone by the Lions management long before departure from the UK and even some of his best form was never going to give him a look-in. But he could have played a valuable supporting role to Hill and Back until a casual knee in the back of Wallabies prop Nic Stiles landed him a two-match ban. After that, like many others among the dirt-trackers, his confidence seemed to evaporate. A keen socialiser and often good company, the Welshman had, however, far too many reasons for simply drowning his sorrows.

BEN COHEN (Northampton and England):
Age 22. Played 4, tries 2, total 10.

The man considered by Clive Woodward to be a better bet than Jason Robinson on the England wing, Cohen certainly had the physical attributes and deceptive pace. But his usual confidence and self-belief seemed to be missing from day one of the tour and, although he produced a reasonable performance in the ACT Brumbies game, his defensive liabilities were startling at times and from mid-tour he sank into the shadows, another peripheral figure ready to bemoan the mantra of the suppressed: the lack of Lions opportunities.

170

MARTIN CORRY (Leicester and England):
Age 27. Played 7 (1 as sub).

Omitted from the original elite thirty-seven, but then drafted in from England's tour of Canada to replace Simon Taylor in the first week, Corry's was one of the most valuable contributions of the whole tour and, while others complained about the lack of opportunities, the Leicester man could have made a serious case for claiming overtime pay. With his knock-knees and comparatively skinny legs, Corry looks an unlikely athlete, but in fact managed to be dynamic, aggressive and adaptable. His ability to win line-out ball at the tail also proved a boon. Played a leading role in the obliteration of the Wallabies back row in the First Test and was promptly dropped to the bench. The story of his England life, too.

LAWRENCE DALLAGLIO (Wasps and England):
Age 28. Played 2.

Alas poor Lawrence, we knew him well. Once as the outstanding England No 8 and so-confident Lion of 1997 and the man thought likely to walk into the Test teams against Australia and then the sad, fretting figure Down Under, wondering where the next game was going to come from. Injured in the end-of-season Zurich play-offs, Dallaglio was almost literally carried around Australia in the hope that he would recover, but in the end he never did. The two games he did play revealed a pale imitation of the great man and it was almost a relief – although the media undoubtedly missed his obliging presence – when he left for home.

JEREMY DAVIDSON (Casters and Ireland):
Age 25. Played 5 (2 as sub).

Four years is a long time in rugby as the South African hero of 1997 discovered. Although everyone knew there was

171

basically only one place available alongside Martin Johnson in the second row, Davidson's frenetic training ability and form as captain of his French club could not get him even close. Suffered, like Scott Murray and Malcolm O'Kelly, from some wayward throwing in by various hookers, but the ability of Danny Grewcock to get around the park made the other locks also-rans and by the end of the tour it was difficult to coax even a smile from normally the most cheerful of men.

MATT DAWSON (Northampton and England):
Age 28. Played 7 (3 as sub), conversions 6,
penalties 3, total 21.

Never likely to threaten the Test starting place of scrum-half Rob Howley, Dawson nevertheless was always likely to be well used, either as cover for the Welshman or the Tuesday No 9. In the event, he was with Corry the busiest player on tour. The most vocal of the dissidents later on Dawson's Diary proved an interesting diversion for everyone with an interest in that sort of thing. But his injury-time conversion of Austin Healey's equalising try against the Brumbies was almost as big a highlight as his indiscretions in print.

SCOTT GIBBS (Swansea and Wales):
Age 30. Played 2, tries 1, total 5.

The man-of-the-series for the Lions in South Africa in 1997, his stuttering Welsh form in the Six Nations could not buy him a spot this time, but obviously in hindsight he should have gone in place of Catt. Arrived in the end like the man on the white charger, but by then Henderson had established himself. Played a couple of games to remind us of past glories, but like a lot of other events on the tour it came far too late.

WILL GREENWOOD (Harlequins and England):
Age 28. Played 4, tries 1, total 5.

A frightening injury and a brush with death sent him home early in 1997 and the luckless Lancastrian did not fare much better this time around, suffering an ankle ligament injury in the New South Wales game that left him on crutches. A pity, because in these days of crash-bang centres Greenwood was a refreshing throwback to the good old days when guile and the ability to break up play was considered essential to midfield play. He had also answered most of the question marks over his defence and none could argue that this was a severe loss.

DANNY GREWCOCK (Bath and England):
Age 28. Played 6, tries 1, total 5.

Showed a relish for the close-quarters stuff that overstepped the mark at times, but Martin Johnson's partner in the second row of the scrum was also highly mobile and, like his captain, one of the game's great grafters. In theory the place alongside Johnson was up for grabs but by the time the First Test came around there was only one real candidate. Went off the boil after that and was badly eclipsed in the deciding match in Sydney against the rejuvenated John Eales and the abrasive rookie Justin Harrison.

AUSTIN HEALEY (Leicester and England):
Age 27. Played 6 (3 as sub), tries 4, total 20.

The most versatile player in the party by a long chalk and also the most controversial by a similar margin, Healey featured in some of the tour's most memorable moments as well as some of the most unsavoury. The best, and worst, of Healey was seen in the ACT Brumbies game where he began his personal feud with Justin Harrison

– a war that he and the Lions lost – but also won the match with two cheeky tries. A man who could cover at scrum-half, stand-off or on the wing, Healey offered options to the management they could not spurn, but this inability to function simply as a specialist does have a price. Like a decathlete, a jack-of-all-trades and master of none.

ROB HENDERSON (Munster and Ireland):
Age 28. Played 6 (1 as sub), tries 4, total 20.

The barrel-chested Irishman was seen as a potent counter to the similarly blockbusting Wallaby centres Nathan Grey and Daniel Herbert, but in fact took them by surprise with some unexpected guile. They had wised up by the Third Test, but in the First in particular he posed problems with Brian O'Driscoll they simply could not handle. Off the field, Henderson is said to be a reformed character but still managed to be the life and soul of the party and a breath of fresh air in this dour era of professional rugby automatons. Fine player, dream interviewee, great company.

RICHARD HILL (Saracens and England):
Age 27. Played 5 (1 as sub), tries 1, total 5.

Most good judges had rated Hill the most underrated forward in world rugby for some time, but on this tour there were no arguments – he was arguably the key man for the Lions alongside Johnson. Although by no means massive in modern back-row terms, Hill still managed to combine pace and formidable strength and commitment, as George Smith would undoubtedly testify after the First Test in Brisbane where the Wallaby flanker was simply overpowered in the loose. Strangely, Henry then stuck him back on the blindside for the Second Test and a cynical assault by Nathan Grey then ended his tour – and the Lions hopes of winning the series.

TYRONE HOWE (Ulster and Ireland):
Age 30. Played 1.

A late arrival in international terms, Howe had only made his international debut for Ireland the year previously at the age of 29 and when arriving on tour as a replacement for Dan Luger had won only six caps. The natural stand-in for Luger had appeared to be his Irish team-mate Denis Hickie, but apparently Hickie was not everyone's cup of tea, particularly the Lions manager Donal Lenihan. Howe played one undistinguished game straight off the plane against the NSW Country XV and never got another chance.

ROB HOWLEY (Cardiff and Wales):
Age 29. Played 4, tries 2, total 10.

The Wales scrum-half's 1997 tour of South Africa had been ended by a shoulder injury before the Tests; this time it was the ribs that took him out in Melbourne. These sort of setbacks seem to have characterised the career of a man who lost his Welsh place and the captaincy at the insistence of the national coach Graham Henry. Howley, however, is not only a superb athlete and a class act, but a dogged battler and by the time the Lions selection came around he was first choice again. Outplayed George Gregan in the First Test; Gregan came good again once Howley disappeared into the treatment room.

DAFYDD JAMES (Llanelli and Wales):
Age 25. Played 7 (1 as sub), tries 3, total 15.

Welsh pundits had reckoned that James would be one of the surprise packets on the tour and they were proved half-right, the injury to Luger, James's dogged perseverance and the poor form of Ben Cohen giving him a place in all three Tests. James has his limitations, in particular a lack of outright pace and vision and his habit of turning away from support cost a try at a vital point in Melbourne. Still, he managed to keep Joe Roff relatively quiet in the First Test and scored a try of his own before the Wallaby wing cut loose in the second. James also provided welcome, if uninspiring, cover in the centre, where at least he could offer sterling defence.

NEIL JENKINS (Cardiff and Wales):
Age 30. Played 4 (1 as sub), conversions 10,
penalties 4, total 32.

Jenkins had virtually won a series in 1997, but the decision to take him to Australia when he was carrying an injury did no favours to his legion of fans or even the player himself. The game's leading scorer with well over 1,000 points, his skills with the boot and passing ability had always outweighed his liabilities, such as his tackling. But Jenkins was exposed badly in Australia, particularly in the Australia A game where he was targeted as the Lions weak point in midfield and where his defensive frailties and lack of pace were shown up badly. With Jonny Wilkinson considered first-choice kicking stand-off anyway, it was a sad end to a great Lions career.

MARTIN JOHNSON (Leicester and England):
Age 30, Played 5.

The first man to captain the Lions on consecutive tours, Johnson again demonstrated that for commitment, leadership and sheer inspiration there was no one to come close to him in world rugby. The sight of him appearing for the first time on tour – against Queensland – was memorably uplifting and said virtually everything about his singular impact on this side. That strange anomaly, a professional rugby player who does it for fun, Johnson also proved a remarkable presence off the field, virtually holding the tour together single-handedly in the last desperate fortnight. Surprisingly media-friendly, and far less frightening than legend would suggest.

JASON LEONARD (Harlequins and England):
Age 32. Played 7 (5 as sub).

The most-capped prop in world rugby was midway through a remarkable Indian summer with England when he received the call from the Lions and the ticket for his third tour. Leonard's evergreen abilities at loose-head – and the fact that he could cover on the other side of the scrum – made him a priceless asset and earned two Test places on the bench before being ousted by Darren Morris in the third. The archetypal tourist – cheerful, friendly and supportive – Leonard was definitely one of the boys. Which of course makes him another modern rugby anachronism.

DAN LUGER (Saracens and England):
Age 26. Played 2, tries 4, total 20.

The former Australian coach Bob Dwyer spouted a lot of tosh throughout the tour, but when he said of Luger that 'you can't afford to lose your first-choice players' he hit the nail on the head for once. Luger was on fire when arriving in Australia and showed in his two appearances that for pace allied with power he ranked alongside the top wings in the world. A training-ground accident and a fractured cheekbone ended all that and the Lions had to go with the less potent Dafydd James. A Luger and Jason Robinson wing combination may just have given the Australians some food for thought.

ROBIN MCBRYDE (Llanelli and Wales):
Age 30. Played 4 (2 as sub).

It was a bad tour for hookers, and none suffered more

than the former Wales Strongest Man. His role was always going to be that of cover for Keith Wood in any case, but picked up a knock in the second game against the Queensland President's XV and never really recovered. Against Australia A in any case he had a cringe-making game and couldn't hit his jumpers in the line-out. Another injury and early departure confirmed that for McBryde this was a tour to forget.

DARREN MORRIS (Swansea and Wales):
Age 26. Played 6 (3 as sub).

After Phil Vickery the heaviest man in the party, Morris could not find Vickery's mobility and even a below-par Tom Smith was still enough to keep him out of Test reckoning at loose-head. Said to be a student of ballet, which made him an interesting concept in propping terms, Morris did show quick feet and hands in the game against Brumbies, helping to set up the last-minute try for Austin Healey, but any higher hopes had vanished in the game against NSW Waratahs where he was badly shown up in the tight.

SCOTT MURRAY (Saracens and Scotland):
Age 25. Played 5 (2 as sub).

One of only three Scots on tour, Murray's previous performances in the Six Nations – particularly in the Calcutta Cup win over England at Murrayfield in 2000 – had given rise to hopes north of the Border that the former basketball player could challenge for the one place free at lock. In the end Murray was a pale shadow of the great athlete and line-out pirate of the previous two seasons and his cause was not helped by the eclipse of the tourists' pack in the game against Australia A. At times seemed worn down by the enormity of it all.

BRIAN O'DRISCOLL (Leinster and Ireland):
Age 22. Played 6, tries 4, total 20.

The one Lions back considered capable of destroying the opposition single-handedly, O'Driscoll was also one of the few to live up to his advance billing and inevitably ended the tour as one of its stars. With a game based on the sort of self-belief that wouldn't go amiss in an Australian side, the Leinster centre had virtually every other attribute of a world-class player, too, with crackling pace, vision, power and underrated defence. A neck injury in the Second Test seemed to take the edge off his game, though, and in the Third attempted to take far too much on himself.

RONAN O'GARA (Munster and Ireland):
Age 24. Played 3 (1 as sub), conversions 13, total 26.

Earned a place on his kicking ability and then was hardly used in that role, except in the first-game devastation of Western Australia. This caused a few mutterings among Scottish judges who had considered Gregor Townsend a more realistic option. Showed some good touches with the ball in hand but really too lightweight at this level and without pace to compensate. As it was, O'Gara will probably be best remembered for the brutal assault on him in Sydney Football Stadium and the pictures of his bloody face which went around the world.

MALCOLM O'KELLY (Leinster and Ireland):
Age 26. Played 4 (1 as sub), tries 1, total 5.

Started the tour with a bang and a try, but was then taken to the cleaners in the Australia A match in Gosford and it all went pear-shaped after that. Marginalised from then on, O'Kelly could well have been sent home suffering from the rife Unwanted Lock Syndrome, such was his impact on

179

the rest of the tour. A pity, because he is obviously a fine athlete.

MATT PERRY (Bath and England):
Age 24, Played 6 (1 as sub), tries 1, conversions 4, total 13.

An example to all that hard work and perseverance will often compensate for lack of outright ability, Perry started the tour as alleged understudy to Iain Balshaw and ended up playing in all three Tests as Balshaw subsided into something close to ignominy. With his laboured running style and lack of pace Perry isn't everyone's cup of tea, but none can question his courage and competence and his intelligent intrusion into the line in the First Test proved crucial for Jason Robinson, who was given the time and space to score the opening try. Perry also proved a fine, cheery tourist.

SCOTT QUINNELL (Llanelli and Wales):
Age 28. Played 6, tries 4, total 20.

One of the tour successes, Quinnell might not quite last the full 80 minutes, or even a whole series; but the damage he can do in an hour or so can be awesome. Certainly in the First Test Australia had no answer to the Llanelli captain and his ability to get past the gain line consistently and never has the great Toutai Kefu looked so impotent. Another player whose South African tour was cut short and whose physical make-up had been called into question in the past, Quinnell had points to prove this time and managed to make most of them.

JASON ROBINSON (Sale and England):
Age 26. Played 7 (1 as sub), tries 10, total 50.

Began the year on the England bench and not even selected in the original sixty-seven players to tour, but came home the most respected, feared and lauded Lion. Used ludicrously as a late-game impact player by England, the Lions management gave him his head from the start and he responded in style. A quiet, modest type off the field, befitting one who receives his guidance from 'up there', Robinson was electric on it and his opening try in the First Test set up a consummate victory and remains one of the tour's great memories. The Australian full-back Chris Latham, of course, would probably prefer to forget the moment 'Billy Whiz' left him on his backside in the Gabba corner.

TOM SMITH (Northampton and Scotland):
Age 29. Played 6 (1 as sub).

After being written off as a Test candidate four years previously and playing in all three, Smith must have had a sense of déjà vu when on arrival in Australia he was immediately written off for the Wallaby tests. Smith, the quiet man of world rugby, immediately set about doing what he does best – letting deeds speak louder than words and comprehensively saw off the challenge of Darren Morris. Had a few hiccups, noticeably against Queensland, but his work ethic and ball-playing skills saw him home in the end.

MARK TAYLOR (Swansea and Wales):
Age 28. Played 5 (2 as sub), tries 2, total 10.

A favourite of Henry and the preferred option to club captain Scott Gibbs, Taylor had a lot to live up to. In the end he didn't do a lot wrong, being a centre in the Australian mould: big, strong and defensively destructive without a lot of pace. But the Ireland pairing at 12 and 13 was always going to be hard to break up and Taylor couldn't make a significant impact. Despite his lack of opportunity, the Welshman stuck it out to the end without whingeing and was a popular tourist.

181

SIMON TAYLOR (Edinburgh and Scotland):
Age 21. Played 1, tries 1, total 5.

Taylor made an instant impression in the forty minutes he played in Perth, scoring one try, making another for Balshaw and producing some class touches, including a classy, reverse spin pass at one point. Not bad for a back-row forward. But that was it, the tour ended there and then with a freak injury and he was badly missed. At twenty-one, it is tempting to say that time is on his side, but that will be small consolation.

PHIL VICKERY (Gloucester and England):
Age 25. Played 6.

The Lions front-row enforcer impressed as he had done all season with his athleticism, support play and work rate but proved curiously less than dominant in the traditional aspects of tight-head play and only occasionally disrupted his opposite number Nic Stiles and the Wallaby scrum. With Grewcock formed a formidable Lions tag team when the red mists came down and paid the price for that on occasions, notably in the horrible Waratahs game and the First Test, being yellow-carded in both games.

DAVID WALLACE (Munster and Ireland):
Age 25. Played 2 (1 as sub), tries 1, total 5.

The third Wallace brother to win a Lions jersey, the flanker had made a forcible impression in the Six Nations pre-tour, but admitted himself he would struggle to have more than a peripheral role to play in Australia. In the end he scored one try on one of his two appearances and off the field proved a friendly, engaging soul and one of the few Lions players to look as though he actually enjoyed touring.

DORIAN WEST (Leicester and England):
Age 33. Played 1.

West swapped the beaches of Minorca for the beaches of Manly when he was plucked from a family holiday as hooker cover. Immediately earned a place on the bench for the Third Test in place of the severely disillusioned Scot Gordon Bulloch, but Wood lasted the pace and the Englishman never got on. The justification for this was that West was up to speed with the English defence formations and spent large parts of the Six Nations throwing in to Grewcock and Johnson. If that was the case, why wasn't he taken along in the first place?

JONNY WILKINSON (Newcastle and England):
Age 22. Played 5, tries 2, conversions 13, penalties 12, total 72.

Inevitably the Lions top-scorer, Wilkinson will still be gnashing his teeth over his miserable success rate with the boot in the Tests, although the much lighter Australian ball was said not to be to his liking. While the rest of the party complained about the hefty training regime, Wilkinson had to be dragged off the practice park on occasions and he above all enhanced his reputation as one of the most dedicated young sportsmen in any game. Injured almost inevitably in the Second Test with one kamikaze tackle too many on the much heavier Daniel Herbert, Wilkinson offered testimony, too, to his massive powers of recuperation by reaching full fitness in six days. Incredible, and hard to credit he is only just twenty-two.

MARTYN WILLIAMS (Cardiff and Wales):
Age 25. Played 4.

A wild card selection, presumably by his Wales coach

Henry, Williams impressed with his work rate in the mid-week sides and forced his way on to the Test bench in the absence of his banned international team-mate, Charvis. Quick and aggressive and another of the non-complainers about his so-sad lot, it was thought that Williams would come out of the tour a far better player. Good news for Henry, then.

KEITH WOOD (Munster and Ireland):
Age 29. Played 6.

Only just shaded by Johnson in the inspirational stakes, Wood also proved a mighty presence in the loose where he buzzed up and down like an auxiliary flanker doing his best to get under Wallaby skins. Son of a Lion, Wood needed little in terms of motivation to get him going and took his role of Johnson's deputy so seriously he abandoned the habit of a lifetime to run out second instead of last. Hard to fault him as a player, and a tourist, although perhaps someone should take him on one side sometime and spend a few training sessions showing him how to throw.

DAI YOUNG (Cardiff and Wales):
Age 33. Played 4, tries 2, total 10.

Amazing to think that Young had made his Test debut for Wales 14 years previously, had toured with the 1989 Lions and was still giving every indication of going on for ever. Lumbered as captain with the midweek moaners, Young simply knuckled down, showed them how to train and play and be a Lion. Should have played a bigger role in the Tests in some eyes, if only as a forty-minute option, but in terms of enhancing a reputation Young didn't do an awful lot wrong. A good last hurrah.

Appendix Two

THE TOUR IN DETAIL

Match One, June 8: Western Australia 10, British and Irish Lions 116 (at the WACA).

Western Australia: Tries: Becroft, Braugh

Lions: Tries: Quinnell 3, Howley 2, Luger 3, Greenwood, Back 2, Grewcock, M Taylor, S Taylor, Balshaw 2, Healey, O'Driscoll. Con: O'Gara 13

(Half-time: 0–57)

Western Australia: Shannon Apaapa, Mark Gardiner, Aaron Broughton, Hamish Waldin, Brent Becroft, Todd Feather, Mark Fleet, Anthony Brian, Richard Coney, Hamish Grace, Trefor Thomas (capt.), Nathan Hollis, Tim Stevens, Campbell Duff, Dirk Gleghorn

Lions: Brian O'Driscoll, Ben Cohen, Will Greenwood, Mark Taylor, Dan Luger, Ronan O'Gara, Rob Howley, Scott Quinnell, Neil Back, Richard Hill, Malcom O'Kelly, Danny Grewcock, Phil Vickery, Keith Wood (capt.), Darren Morris

Match 2, June 12: Queensland Presidents XV 6, British and Irish Lions 83 (at Dairy Farmers Stadium, Townsville).

Queensland Presidents XV: Pen: Drahm 2

Lions: Tries: Young, Charvis 2, Robinson 5, Henderson 3, O'Kelly

Con: Jenkins 5, Perry 4

(Half-time: 6–10)

Queensland Presidents XV: Nathan Williams, David McCallum, Junior Pelesasa, Jason Ramsamy, Scott Barton, Shane Drahm, Ben Wakely, John Roe, Scott Fava, Tom McVerry, Rudi Vedelayo, Mike Mitchell, Fletcher Dyson, Sean Hardman, Ricky Tyrell

Lions: Matt Perry, Daffyd James, Will Greenwood, Rob Henderson, Jason Robinson, Neil Jenkins, Matt Dawson, Martin Corry, Martyn Williams, Colin Charvis, Scott Murray, Jeremy Davidson, Dai Young (capt.), Robin McBryde, Tom Smith

Match 3, June 16: Queensland Reds 8, British and Irish Lions 42 (at Ballymore).

Queensland Reds: Tries: Cordingley. Pen: Flatley

Lions: Tries: Luger, Henderson, James, Hill, O'Driscoll

Con: Wilkinson 4

Pen: Wilkinson 4

(Half-time: 3–32)

Queensland Reds: Michael Tabrett, Junior Pelesasa, Daniel Herbert (capt.), Steve Kefu, David McCallum, Elton Flatley, Sam Cordingley, Toutai Kefu, David Croft, Matt Cockbain, Mark Connors, Nathan Sharpe, Glenn Panoho, Michael Foley, Nick Stiles

Lions: Iain Balshaw, Dafydd James, Brian O'Driscoll, Rob Henderson, Dan Luger, Jonny Wilkinson, Rob Howley, Martin Corry, Neil Back, Richard Hill, Danny Grewcock, Martin Johnson (capt.), Phil Vickery, Keith Wood, Tom Smith

Match 4, June 19: Australia A 28, British and Irish Lions 25 (at North Power Stadium, Gosford).

Australia A: Try: Staniforth. Con: Edmonds. Pen: Edmonds 7

Lions: Tries: Taylor, Perry, Robinson. Con: Dawson 2. Pen: Jenkins 2

(Half-time: 15–6)

Australia A: Richard Graham, Mark Bartholomeusz, Graeme Bond, Nathan Grey, Scott Staniforth, Manuel Edmonds, Chris Whitaker, Jim Williams, Phil Waugh (capt.), David Lyons, Justin Harrison, Brendan Cannon, Tom Bowman, Rod Moore, Cameron Blades

Lions: Matt Perry, Ben Cohen, Will Greenwood, Mike Catt, Jason Robinson, Neil Jenkins, Austin Healey, Scott Quinnell, Martyn Williams, Lawrence Dallaglio, Malcolm O'Kelly, Scott Murray, Dai Young (capt.), Robin McBryde, Jason Leonard

Match 5, June 23: New South Wales Waratahs 24, British and Irish Lions 41 (at Sydney Football Stadium).

NSW Waratahs: Tries: Pinkerton, Cullimore, Harris, Edmonds. Con: Edmonds 2

Lions: Tries: O'Driscoll, Robinson 2, Wilkinson, James. Con: Wilkinson 4. Pen: Wilkinson 2, Dawson

(Half-time: 5–24)

NSW Waratahs: Duncan McRae, Francis Cullimore, Luke Inman, Sam Harris, Sikeli Qau Qau, Manuel Edmonds, Sam Payne, Fili Finau, Phil Waugh (capt.), Stu Pinkerton,

Tom Bowman, Jono West, Rod Moore, Brendan Cannon, Cameron Blades.

Lions: Iain Balshaw, Dafydd James, Brian O'Driscoll, Will Greenwood, Jason Robinson, Jonny Wilkinson, Matt Dawson, Scott Quinnell, Neil Back, Lawrence Dallaglio, Danny Grewcock, Martin Johnson (capt.), Phil Vickery, Keith Wood, Darren Morris

Match 6, June 26: New South Wales Country XV 3, British and Irish Lions 46 (at International Stadium, Coffs Harbour).

NSW Country: Pen: Croft

Lions: Tries: Cohen 2, Charvis, Gibbs, Healey, Young. Con: Jenkins 5. Pen: Jenkins 2

(Half-time: 3–29)

NSW Country: N Croft; V Tailasa, R Macdougall, K Shepherd, W Crosby, C Doyle, R Petty, A Baldwin, J McCormack, M Bowman, D Lubans, B Wright, B Dale, C Taylor, B Klasen

Lions: Iain Balshaw, Ben Cohen, Mark Taylor, Scott Gibbs, Tyrone Howe, Neil Jenkins, Austin Healey, Martin Corry, Colin Charvis, Martyn Williams, Malcolm O'Kelly, Jeremy Davidson, David Young (capt.), Gordon Bulloch, Jason Leonard

Match 7, June 30: Australia 13, British and Irish Lions 29 (at The Gabba, Brisbane).

Australia: Tries: Walker, Grey. Pen: Walker

Lions: Tries: Robinson, James, O'Driscoll, Quinnell. Con: Wilkinson 3. Pen: Wilkinson

(Half-time: 3–12)

Australia: Chris Latham, Andrew Walker, Daniel Herbert, Nathan Grey, Joe Roff, Stephen Larkham, George Gregan, Toutai Kefu, George Smith, Owen Finegan, John Eales (capt.), David Giffin, Glenn Panoho, Jeremy Paul, Nick Stiles.

Replacements: Michael Foley, Ben Darwin, Matt Cockbain, David Lyons, Chris Whitaker, Elton Flatley, Matthew Burke

Lions: Matt Perry, Dafydd James, Brian O'Driscoll, Rob Henderson, Jason Robinson, Jonny Wilkinson, Rob Howley, Scott Quinnell, Richard Hill, Martin Corry, Danny Grewcock, Martin Johnson (capt.), Phil Vickery, Keith Wood, Tom Smith

Replacements: Gordon Bulloch, Jason Leonard, Colin Charvis, Martyn Williams, Matt Dawson, Austin Healey, Iain Balshaw.

Referee: André Watson (South Africa)

Match 8, July 3: ACT Brumbies 28, British and Irish Lions 30 (at Bruce Stadium, Canberra).

ACT Brumbies: Tries: Bartholomeusz, Gordon, Tuiavii. Con: Hall 2. Pen: Hall 3

Lions: Tries: Healey 2, D Wallace. Con: Dawson 3. Pen: Dawson 2

(Half-time: 22–10)

ACT Brumbies: Mark Bartholomeusz, Damien McInally,

Graeme Bond, James Holbeck, Willie Gordon, Pat Howard, Travis Hall, Jim Williams (capt.), Des Tuiavii, Daniel Vickerman, Peter Ryan, Justin Harrison, Matt Weaver, Adam Freier, Angus Scott

Lions: Iain Balshaw, Ben Cohen, Mark Taylor, Scott Gibbs, Austin Healey, Ronan O'Gara, Matt Dawson, Martin Corry, Martyn Williams, David Wallace, Scott Murray, Jeremy Davidson, David Young (capt.), Dorian West, Darren Morris

Match 9, July 7: Australia 35, British and Irish Lions 14 (at Colonial Stadium, Melbourne).

Australia: Tries: Roff 2, Burke. Con: Burke. Pen: Burke 6

Lions: Tries: Back. Pen: Wilkinson 3.

(Half-time: 6–11)

Australia: Matthew Burke, Andrew Walker, Daniel Herbert, Nathan Grey, Joe Roff, Stephen Larkham, George Gregan, Toutai Kefu, George Smith, Owen Finegan, John Eales (capt.), David Giffin, Rod Moore, Michael Foley, Nick Stiles

Replacements: Chris Latham, Elton Flatley, Brendan Cannon, Matt Cockbain, Ben Darwin, David Lyons, Chris Whitaker.

Lions: Matt Perry, Dafydd James, Brian O'Driscoll, Rob Henderson, Jason Robinson, Jonny Wilkinson, Rob Howley, Scott Quinnell, Neil Back, Richard Hill, Danny Grewcock, Martin Johnson (capt.), Phil Vickery, Keith Wood, Tom Smith

Replacements: Iain Balshaw, Neil Jenkins, Matt Dawson for Howley, Jason Leonard, Martin Corry, Dorian West, Martyn Williams

Referee: Jonathan Kaplan (South Africa)

Match 10, July 14: Australia 29, British and Irish Lions 23 (at Stadium Australia, Sydney).

Australia: Tries: Herbert 2. Con: Burke 2. Pen: Burke 5

Lions: Tries: Robinson, Wilkinson. Con: Wilkinson 2. Pen: Wilkinson 3

Australia: Matt Burke, Andrew Walker, Daniel Herbert, Nathan Grey, Joe Roff, Elton Flatley, George Gregan, Toutai Kefu, George Smith, Owen Finegan, John Eales (capt.), Justin Harrison, Rod Moore, Michael Foley, Nick Stiles

Replacements: Brendan Cannon, Ben Darwin, Matt Cockbain, David Lyons, Chris Whitaker, James Holbeck, Chris Latham

Lions: Matt Perry, Dafydd James, Brian O'Driscoll, Rob Henderson, Jason Robinson, Jonny Wilkinson, Matt Dawson, Scott Quinell, Neil Back, Martin Corry, Martin Johnson (capt.), Danny Grewcock, Phil Vickery, Keith Wood, Tom Smith

Replacements: Darren Morris, Dorian West, Colin Charvis, Martyn Williams Ronan O'Gara, Andy Nicol, Iain Balshaw

Referee: Paddy O'Brien (New Zealand)

Total: P10, W7, L3. Points for 449, against 184

Top points scorers: 72 – Jonny Wilkinson, 50 – Jason Robinson, 32 – Neil Jenkins, 26 – Ronan O'Gara, 21 – Matt Dawson

Top try scorers: 10 – Jason Robinson, 4 – Austin Healey, Rob

191

Henderson, Dan Luger, Brian O'Driscoll, Scott Quinnell, 3 – Neil Back, Colin Charvis, Dafydd James

Place kicking percentage: Matt Perry 100% (4/4), Neil Jenkins 74% (14/19), Ronan O'Gara 72% (13/18), Jonny Wilkinson 71% (25/35), Matt Dawson 64% (9/14)

Most appearances: (starts only) 6 – Martin Corry, Danny Grewcock, Dafydd James, Brian O'Driscoll, Scott Quinnell, Jason Robinson, Phil Vickery, Keith Wood, 5 – Neil Back, Rob Henderson, Martin Johnson, Matt Perry, Tom Smith, Jonny Wilkinson

Most appearances as substitute: 5 – Jason Leonard, 4 – Iain Balshaw, Colin Charvis